Around the World
Cookbook

AROUND the WORLD
COOKBOOK

by Abigail Johnson Dodge

DK Publishing

LONDON, NEW YORK, MELBOURNE,
MUNICH, AND DELHI

Senior Editor Elizabeth Hester
Designer Bill Miller
Managing Art Editor Michelle Baxter
Art Director Dirk Kaufman
DTP Coordinator Kathy Farias
Production Manager Ivor Parker
Publishing Director Beth Sutinis

Photography by Tina Rupp

DOWNTOWN
BOOKWORKS INC.

PRODUCED BY DOWNTOWN BOOKWORKS INC.
President Julie Merberg
Senior Vice President Patty Brown
Editor Sara Newberry

First American Edition, 2008

Published in the United States by
DK Publishing
375 Hudson Street, New York, New York 10014
10 11 12 10 9 8 7 6 5 4
SD335—July 2008
Copyright © 2008 Dorling Kindersley Limited
Text copyright © 2008
Downtown Bookworks Inc. and Abigail Johnson Dodge
All rights reserved.

A catalog record for this book is available from
the Library of Congress.
ISBN 978-0-7566-3744-6

DK books are available at special discounts
when purchased in bulk for sales promotions,
premiums, fundraising, or educational use.
For details, contact: DK Publishing Special Markets,
375 Hudson Street, New York, New York 10014
or SpecialSales@dk.com.

Color Reproduction by Colourscan, Singapore
Printed and bound in China by Leo Paper Products Ltd.

Discover more at
www.dk.com

CONTENTS

8 THE BASICS: GETTING STARTED

The Kitchen • Gather Your Gear! • Learn the Lingo • Working with Ingredients • Sharp-Tool Skills • Power-Tool Skills • The End of the Road

20 ASIA

Salmon Teriyaki • Miso Soup • Bok Choy Stir-Fry • Vegetable Fried Rice • Shrimp Pad Thai • Vietnamese Lettuce Rolls

32 INDIA, INDONESIA, AND AUSTRALASIA

Lemony Lamb Skewers • ANZAC Biscuits • Pavlova • Tandoori Chicken Legs • Cauliflower and Pea Curry

44 Pocket Food Around the World

How to Use This Book

Welcome to *Around the World Cookbook*. You're about to learn to cook your way around the globe! In this book, along with lots of great recipes, you'll find a world of information about food, culture, and more. There are a few different kinds of pages in the book, and it's useful to know what kind of information you'll see on each one. Here's a first look at the road ahead.

Not sure how to mince or dice or shred? Turn to Basics (pages 8–19) for step-by-step directions and helpful photos. You'll also learn about kitchen safety, tools, and other cooking tips in this section.

Basic skills

At the start of each chapter, you will find a map and photo of the region, as well as useful information about the part of the world included in that chapter.

You are here!

Special feature maps throughout the book show you how one kind of food appears in many cultures. You'll be amazed by how much we have in common!

Food around the world

The Recipes

You'll find the recipe's name and its country of origin here.

This list tells you the tools you'll need to follow the recipe.

These are the steps of the recipe. This is what you'll do to make the dish.

Learn a little about the dish and the place it comes from here.

Look here for more information about ingredients, cooking styles, and places.

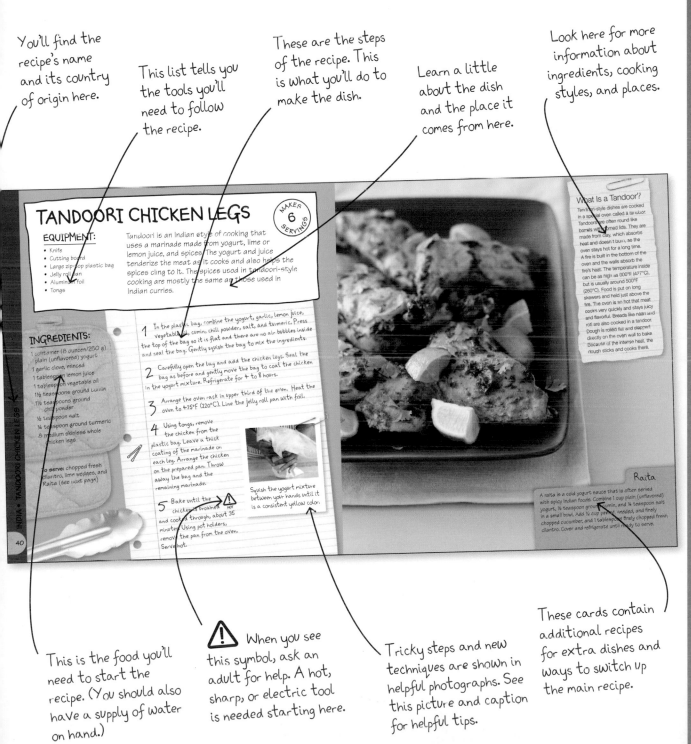

TANDOORI CHICKEN LEGS

MAKES 6 SERVINGS

Tandoori is an Indian style of cooking that uses a marinade made from yogurt, lime or lemon juice, and spices. The yogurt and juice tenderize the meat as it cooks and also helps the spices cling to it. The spices used in tandoori-style cooking are mostly the same as those used in Indian curries.

EQUIPMENT:
- Knife
- Cutting board
- Large zip-top plastic bag
- Jelly roll pan
- Aluminum foil
- Tongs

INGREDIENTS:
- 1 container (8 ounces/250 g) plain (unflavored) yogurt
- 1 garlic clove, minced
- 1 tablespoon lemon juice
- 1 tablespoon vegetable oil
- 1½ teaspoons ground cumin
- 1½ teaspoons ground chili powder
- ½ teaspoon salt
- ¼ teaspoon ground turmeric
- 8 medium skinless whole chicken legs

To serve: chopped fresh cilantro, lime wedges, and Raita (see next page)

1. In the plastic bag, combine the yogurt, garlic, lemon juice, vegetable oil, cumin, chili powder, salt, and turmeric. Press the top of the bag so it is flat and there are no air bubbles inside and seal the bag. Gently squish the bag to mix the ingredients.

2. Carefully open the bag and add the chicken legs. Seal the bag as before and gently move the bag to coat the chicken in the yogurt mixture. Refrigerate for 4 to 8 hours.

3. Arrange the oven rack in upper third of the oven. Heat the oven to 475°F (220°C). Line the jelly roll pan with foil.

4. Using tongs, remove the chicken from the plastic bag. Leave a thick coating of the marinade on each leg. Arrange the chicken on the prepared pan. Throw away the bag and the remaining marinade.

Squish the yogurt mixture between your hands until it is a consistent yellow color.

5. ⚠ Bake until the chicken is browned HOT and cooked through, about 35 minutes. Using pot holders, remove the pan from the oven. Serve hot.

What Is a Tandoor?
Tandoori-style dishes are cooked in a special oven called a tandoor. Tandoors are often round like barrels with domed lids. They are made from clay, which absorbs heat and doesn't burn, so the oven stays hot for a long time. A fire is built in the bottom of the oven and the walls absorb the fire's heat. The temperature inside can be as high as 900°F (477°C), but is usually around 500°F (260°C). Food is put on long skewers and held just above the fire. The oven is so hot that meat cooks very quickly and stays juicy and flavorful. Breads like naan and roti are also cooked in a tandoor. Dough is rolled flat and slapped directly on the oven wall to bake. Because of the intense heat, the dough sticks and cooks there.

Raita
A raita is a cold yogurt sauce that is often served with spicy Indian foods. Combine 1 cup plain (unflavored) yogurt, ½ teaspoon ground cumin, and ¼ teaspoon salt in a small bowl. Add ½ cup peeled, seeded, and finely chopped cucumber, and 1 tablespoon finely chopped fresh cilantro. Cover and refrigerate until ready to serve.

This is the food you'll need to start the recipe. (You should also have a supply of water on hand.)

⚠ When you see this symbol, ask an adult for help. A hot, sharp, or electric tool is needed starting here.

Tricky steps and new techniques are shown in helpful photographs. See this picture and caption for helpful tips.

These cards contain additional recipes for extra dishes and ways to switch up the main recipe.

The Kitchen

Just like taking a trip around the world, exploring new recipes is a lot easier if you prepare before you start. Get to know a recipe before you begin so you don't miss a step. And remember: Nothing is more important than your safety. So be very careful, take your time, and come back to this section often to review safety tips and basic skills. The best journey is a safe one!

Clean hands are a very important tool!

Before You Begin

✓ Always ask an adult for permission before beginning any recipe.

✓ Read through the recipe with an adult. Read it twice to really understand. It helps to read it out loud, too.

✓ Clear a workspace.

✓ Tie hair back.

✓ Wash hands with soap and warm water.

✓ Wear an apron and have a kitchen towel by your side.

✓ Gather all the equipment you'll need.

✓ Carefully measure all ingredients.

✓ Arrange a damp paper towel under your cutting board so it stays in place.

✓ Understand how to tell when a dish is done. (The recipe will tell you how the food will look, smell, or taste when it's ready.)

RULES OF THE ROAD

Helping Hands

- Always ask for an adult's help when you see this symbol: ⚠
- When using a stove or oven, ask an adult for help.
- Have an adult assemble any electrical equipment and help you operate it.
- Always have an adult help when pouring hot liquids. Pour the hot contents away from your body.

Hot Stuff

- Check that pot holders are dry and without holes.
- When removing lids from hot pots, always open and move them away from your body and face.
- Always use pot holders on dishes or pans in the oven and on handles of pots and skillets on the stove.
- When not stirring, turn pot handles away from the edge of the stove.

Lookin' Sharp!

- Only use knives and sharp tools (peelers and graters) with an adult's help.
- Never let any part of a knife dangle over the edge of the work surface. When not in use, position it away from the edge.
- When you are finished with a sharp tool, clean it right away instead of putting it with the other dirty dishes—you don't want to forget and grab it.

GATHER YOUR GEAR!

When you travel, you need your passport, your camera, and your luggage. When you cook, the right equipment is just as important. Check your kitchen for these essential tools.

Chef's knife
A knife used for most kitchen jobs. Larger than a paring knife.

Paring knife
A small knife used for tasks like chopping apples or berries.

Spatula
There are two kinds of spatulas: soft rubber ones for scraping mixing bowls, and rigid ones used to flip food in a skillet.

Slotted spoon
A spoon with holes or slits that hold solids but let liquids drain.

Tongs
A tool used to grab large ingredients while cooking. You can use tongs to turn food in a pan.

Whisk
A tool made from wire bent into a balloon shape. Used to mix food to a light, airy consistency.

Box grater
Used to shred ingredients like cheese, carrots, and potatoes.

Colander
Shaped like a bowl, a colander has holes all over it so that liquid will drain but solid ingredients stay in the bowl.

Skillet
A large flat pan. Foods cook evenly in a skillet because they can be spread out into one layer.

Saucepan
A deep pan usually used to cook liquids like sauces or soups.

Cookie sheet
A flat baking pan. A cookie sheet has just one raised edge, so should be used only for cookies or breads that don't spread very much while they bake.

Jelly roll pan
A flat baking pan with raised edges that keep batter or dough in the pan.

LEARN THE LINGO

Don't forget your phrasebook! Here are some cooking words you'll see in the recipes. Use this list to help you navigate new skills.

Batter
A mixture of flour, liquid, and some fat used in baking. Cakes and pancakes are usually made from batter.

Blend
To mix ingredients so that they look like one ingredient. When a mixture is blended, it is all the same color.

Boil
Water is boiling when the bubbles rise from the bottom of the pan and burst when they reach the surface.

Dough
A mixture of flour, fat, and liquid. A dough is stiffer than a batter and usually needs to be shaped before baking. Most cookies and breads are made from dough.

Fold
Using a rubber spatula to gently lift and turn the ingredients, bringing them from the bottom of the bowl to the top.

Knead
To fold dough over on itself. Kneading helps dough rise when making bread.

Preheat
To turn on the oven before it is needed. This helps to make sure the oven is at the right temperature when the food goes in.

Sauté
To cook food quickly while moving it around in the pan. *Sauté* means "jump" in French.

Simmer
When a liquid is bubbling gently. Liquid simmers before it boils.

Sprinkle
To spread a mixture evenly over another ingredient or a surface. Dry toppings or ingredients like sugar are usually sprinkled.

Toss
Using two tools (like spoons) to lift up ingredients within a mixture. This gently combines and coats by bringing the ingredients on the bottom to the top. Repeat until ingredients are mixed.

Whisk
To use a whisk to stir or combine. Whisking also adds air, giving ingredients more volume than stirring.

WORKING WITH INGREDIENTS

Just like every trip is different, every recipe is different. But they all have one thing in common: you need to prepare your ingredients before you begin. Here are some tips on how to get them ready to go!

Tender-skinned fruit or vegetables (like peaches or zucchini)

1 Rinse under cold tap water.

2 Pat dry with paper towels.

Tough-skinned fruit and vegetables (like potatoes or melons)

1 Rinse under cold tap water and use a vegetable brush to gently rub the skin.

2 Let dry and peel or slice as directed.

Berries and fragile fruits

1 Arrange the fruit in a colander.

2 Pass the colander under cold tap water several times to rinse fruit. Let fruit drain in colander.

3 Spread on paper towels and let dry.

Herbs and salad greens

1 Arrange the greens or herbs in a colander.

2 Pass the colander under cold tap water several times to rinse.

3 Roll up in a paper towel and gently squeeze dry.

Breaking an egg

1 Holding the egg in one hand, tap the shell against the edge of a bowl. The shell will crack slightly.

2 Using both hands, hold the egg over the bowl, cracked side down. Gently pull apart the shell. The yolk and the white will fall into the bowl.

3 Use one half of the shell to scoop out any shell pieces.

Separating egg whites

1 Be extra sure that your bowl is very, very clean. Rinse your bowl with warm water and a splash of white vinegar. (Don't worry, you won't taste the vinegar!) Pour the liquid out. Dry well with a paper towel.

2 Holding the egg in one hand, tap the shell against the edge of a bowl.

3 Hold the egg over the bowl, cracked side UP. Gently pull apart the shell, letting the whites fall into the clean bowl.

4 When all the white has fallen away from the yolk, discard the yolk and shells. Repeat with remaining eggs. (Do not let any of the yolk drip into the whites or they won't beat up properly.)

Measuring dry ingredients

1 Hold a measuring spoon or a dry-measure cup firmly in one hand.

2 Lightly spoon ingredient into cup—do NOT pack down.

3 Run a knife over the rim to level off the top.

Measuring liquids

1 Place cup on a level countertop.

2 Pour liquid into measuring cup.

3 Bend down to check measuring line at eye level.

SHARP-TOOL SKILLS ⚠ SHARP

Just like a camera or a guidebook on a vacation, sharp tools are a necessity on kitchen journeys. Here are some pointers for a safe and successful sojourn. Remember: Ask an adult to supervise.

Shredding cheese or vegetables

1 Put the grater on your work surface with the large shredding holes pointing away from you. Hold the handle with one hand.

2 Keep your fingers back and away from the sharp holes.

3 Holding the end of the block of cheese or vegetable, slowly slide it down the shredder.

Chopping onions

1 Put the onion on the work surface. Cut in half through the stem. Peel away the skin.

2 Position the onion so the stem is against the cutting board.

3 Hold the stem end with your fingertips. Using long strokes, make slices toward the stem. (The stem end will hold the slices together.)

4 Keep holding the stem end. Drag the knife across the slices. Repeat to make chopped pieces.

Dicing bell peppers

1 Put the pepper on the work surface stem side up. Hold one side of the stem end with your fingers. Place the knife on the other side of the stem. Cut down to the bottom.

2 Put the pepper cut side down with the stem away from you. Using a long stroke, cut into a thick slice. Turn and repeat until only the core and bottom remain.

3 Cut each strip into thin slices. Cut each slice into small pieces.

Mincing garlic

1 Break the cloves from the head and place on a work surface.

2 Hit a clove with the side of your fist to crush slightly and break the skin. Peel away the skin.

3 Hold the knife in one hand and the fingers of the other hand flat on top of the blade.

4 Slowly rock the knife back and forth until garlic is in tiny pieces.

Finely chopping fresh herbs

1 Wash and dry herbs. Pluck the leaves off the stems.

2 Pile on the work surface. (Stack large leaves, such as basil.)

3 Hold the knife in one hand and the fingers of the other hand flat on top of the blade.

4 Slowly rock the knife back and forth until the herbs are chopped.

Peeling fruit or vegetables

1 Rinse and dry fruit or vegetable.

2 Hold one end of the fruit or vegetable on your work surface.

3 Slide the peeler from one end to the other. Always move the peeler away from you.

4 Turn and peel until skin is removed.

Coring an apple

1 Place an apple on the work surface stem side up. Cut in half.

2 Using a melon baller or a small spoon, scoop out the center, core, and seeds from each half.

3 Position the halves flat side down. Cut into slices as directed in the recipe.

POWER-TOOL SKILLS ⚠ ELECTRIC

Remember to bring your adapter! Electric tools are not used every time you cook, but enough that you should know how to use them. Remember: Always ask for an adult's permission before using any of these tools.

Food processor

1 Have an adult assemble the food processor. The blade is VERY sharp.

2 Add the ingredients to the processor bowl. Put the lid on and lock in place.

3 With one hand on the top to steady the machine, press the PULSE button. Keep pressing "pulse" until the task is completed as directed in the recipe.

4 Have an adult remove the ingredients from the processor. Continue with the recipe as directed.

Stand mixer

1 With the attachment arm raised, add the ingredients to the mixing bowl.

2 Carefully lower the attachment into the bowl. Lock the arm into place.

3 Turn the mixer on a slow speed, then increase speed as directed in the recipe.

4 Turn the mixer off and wait for the beater to stop moving completely before unlocking the attachment arm.

5 With the mixer off, use a rubber spatula to scrape down the sides of the bowl. NEVER stick your hands or a tool in the mixer while it's running.

Hand-held electric mixer

1 Place a kitchen towel or damp paper towel on work surface. Position a mixing bowl on top so it won't wiggle around. Fill with ingredients as directed.

2 Lock beater attachments into place and plug in the cord.

3 Hold the mixer over the bowl with the beaters completely in bowl. Turn the mixer on low and gradually increase speed as directed. DO NOT lift beaters from bowl when mixer is on or you'll have a big mess!

4 To scrape the sides of the bowl or to check for doneness, turn off the mixer. Wait until the beaters completely stop before lifting them out of the bowl.

5 Use a rubber spatula to scrape down the sides of the bowl.

Blender

1 Add the ingredients to the blender.

2 Put the lid on and snap into place. Cover the top with a kitchen towel.

3 Put one hand on top to steady the machine and hold down the lid. Press "blend" or "medium-high." Blend until smooth or as directed.

THE END OF THE ROAD

Finish each kitchen journey by cleaning up and putting your tools away so your workspace is clean and organized. You'll be ready for your next adventure in no time.

Don't forget to clean up!

- Wipe up any spills or splatters when they happen. Dried spills are harder to clean.

- Put away ingredients and equipment as you use them.

- Use a clean kitchen towel to dry equipment before putting it away.

- Never put knives in a sink full of soapy water! Put them safely to the side of the sink and ask an adult to wash them.

- Let hot pots, skillets, and baking dishes cool completely before cleaning. Let them cool on the stove or cooling rack with a pot holder on the handle before moving them to the sink.

Ready, set...

I hope you're as excited as I am to travel around the world through these recipes. There's so much to learn about what culture, climate, and tradition have to do with dining, and where our favorite flavors come from. And, of course, cooking is a great way to have fun with friends and family! Before you get going, here are a few final tips for the road:

- All stoves and ovens are slightly different. Set your timer to go off a few minutes before a dish is supposed to be done to make sure it doesn't overcook or burn.

- Trust your instincts and your senses. If something doesn't look right, ask an adult for help.

- If you have any questions or problems, always ask an adult for help.

- If you think something on the stove is cooking too fast, turn the heat down. Use pot holders to slide the pot to a cool burner, then continue cooking.

- If something in the oven smells like it is burning, turn off the heat. Use pot holders to move the pan to a cooling rack.

- Work slowly and carefully. It's not a race!

And of course, have fun!
Food seems to taste better
when you've cooked it yourself.

Happy travels,

Abby

Asia

Asia is the world's largest continent, home to more than 50 countries. So it's not surprising that the people and cultures are very different from place to place. Rice grows very well in the rainy climate and is used as an ingredient in many of the dishes. Ginger and garlic are native to the region and also commonly used in Asian cooking.

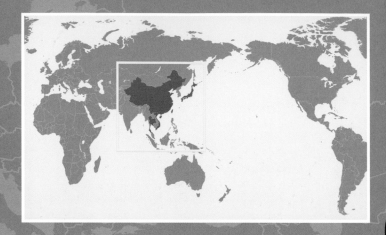

Traditional Japanese architecture at the Daigoji Temple in Kyoto

China

With more than one billion people, China has the highest population of any country on Earth. What you'll eat in China depends on where you are. In the north, steamed buns and noodles are very common. In southern China, rice is the main part of every meal. People use chopsticks to eat most foods except soup, which is eaten with large, flat-bottomed spoons.

Japan

Japan is part of the "Ring of Fire," a group of islands formed by volcanoes in the Pacific Ocean. Because the land is so mountainous, there is very little farming in Japan. Rice is the most common crop and is included with nearly every meal. Japan is surrounded by water, so seafood is eaten more often than meat or poultry. Presentation, or how the food looks on the plate, is very important in Japanese cuisine.

C H I N A

JAPAN

PACIFIC OCEAN

Thailand

Unlike its neighbors Vietnam and Cambodia, Thailand has never been colonized by a European country. And unlike China, Japan, and the rest of Southeast Asia, the Thai people eat most meals with a knife and fork. Thailand is the world's largest exporter of rice—there are more than 5,000 varieties found there. Besides rice, the main element in Thai cooking is the use of five flavors in every dish: sweet, spicy, sour, bitter, and salty.

THAILAND

VIETNAM

Vietnam

Vietnam has spent much of its history as a colony settled by other countries, mainly China and France. Influences from both are seen in Vietnamese food. A favorite street food is *banh mi,* a sandwich made with Asian spices and pâté, a meat paste introduced by French settlers. Another favorite is a noodle soup called *pho.*

INDIAN OCEAN

SALMON TERIYAKI

MAKES
4
SERVINGS

EQUIPMENT:

- Medium bowl
- Whisk
- 12 bamboo or metal skewers
- Wire cooling rack
- Broiler pan
- Aluminum foil
- Small saucepan

Teriyaki is the name of a traditional Japanese cooking style. *Teri* means "glaze" (for the sweet-salty marinade) and *yaki* means "grilling" or "broiling." Fish is commonly prepared this way, but chicken and meat can also be cooked teriyaki-style. Teriyaki dishes are usually served hot, but they're sometimes packed cold in *bento*, or box meals.

INGREDIENTS:

¼ cup soy sauce

2 tablespoons rice wine vinegar or white vinegar

1 tablespoon honey

2 teaspoons minced ginger

½ teaspoon cornstarch

1 pound (450 g) salmon fillet, cut into four 1-inch (2.5-cm)–thick strips

Nonstick cooking spray

To serve: cooked rice

In Step 1: Stir carefully, lifting and turning each piece until coated with sauce.

1 In the medium bowl, whisk together the soy sauce, 3 tablespoons water, vinegar, honey, ginger, and cornstarch. Add the salmon strips and toss gently to coat.

2 Cover and refrigerate 15 minutes. Turn the salmon over in the sauce. Cover and refrigerate 15 more minutes.

3 Arrange the oven rack in the upper third of the oven. Heat the broiler to high. Line the pan with foil and spray with cooking spray.

4 Thread the salmon strips lengthwise onto the skewers. Arrange the salmon, flat side down, on the prepared pan. SAVE the marinade.

5 Broil until the salmon is browned and cooked through, 8 to 10 minutes. Using pot holders, move the pan to the cooling rack. ⚠️ HOT

6 Meanwhile, pour the reserved marinade into the saucepan. Bring to a boil. Boil, stirring frequently, until thick, 1 minute. Serve the salmon over rice with the sauce on the side.

Sushi

Sushi combines two Japanese favorites: seafood and rice. In roll-style sushi (called *maki*), the rice and seafood are rolled up in a thin layer of dried seaweed (*nori*) and sliced. Sushi is usually served with soy sauce, pickled ginger, and a spicy green paste called *wasabi*. Tuna, salmon, and other fish are popular, but sushi bars serve everything from vegetable and cooked-meat *maki* to sea urchin and squid.

MISO SOUP

MAKES
4
SERVINGS

EQUIPMENT:

- Knife
- Cutting board
- Large saucepan
- Small bowl
- Spoon
- Ladle

Most people in Japan eat miso soup at least once a day, often for breakfast. Unlike other soups, miso soup is usually not eaten with a spoon. The solid ingredients are eaten with chopsticks and the broth is drunk directly from the bowl.

INGREDIENTS:

4 shiitake mushrooms
4 cups vegetable broth
4 tablespoons miso paste
4 teaspoons soy sauce
⅓ cup diced firm tofu
2 green onions, trimmed
   and thinly sliced

1   Cut the stems from the mushrooms. Thinly slice the mushrooms.   ⚠ SHARP

2   In the large saucepan, bring the broth to a boil over high heat. Add the sliced mushrooms. Reduce heat to low and simmer 4 minutes.   ⚠ HOT

3   In a small bowl, mix the miso and soy sauce. Stir into the soup along with the tofu. Cook 1 minute. Do not boil.

4   Carefully pour or ladle into serving bowls. Sprinkle with the green onions. Serve right away.

Miso Paste

Miso paste is made of soybeans, salt, and grains. The mixture, called *koji*, is aged in wooden barrels for a few months or as much as two years. The longer miso ages, the stronger and saltier the flavor. Three popular varieties are: *shiro* (pale yellow, with a mild taste); *aka* (dark brown, with a strong, salty flavor); and *shinsyu* (light brown, with a medium flavor).

BOK CHOY STIR-FRY

MAKES
4
SERVINGS

EQUIPMENT:

- Knife
- Cutting board
- Wok or large skillet
- Wooden spoon

Bok choy, or Chinese cabbage, has been used in Chinese cooking for thousands of years. Its sweet, fresh flavor features in some Filipino and Korean dishes, too. The ends of the leaves are too tough to eat, so trim them before cooking the rest.

INGREDIENTS:

- 1 head bok choy
- 2 tablespoons vegetable oil
- 1 red bell pepper, chopped
- 1 garlic clove, minced
- 2 teaspoons minced ginger
- 3 tablespoons soy sauce
- 2 teaspoons sesame oil

1 Separate the bok choy stalks. Cut the green leafy tops into 2-inch (5-cm)–thick slices. Cut the white stalk ends into ¾-inch (2-cm)–thick slices.

⚠ SHARP

2 Heat the oil in the wok over medium-high heat. Add the white stalk slices and pepper pieces. Cook, stirring constantly, until slightly softened, about 3 minutes.

⚠ HOT

3 Add the garlic and ginger. Cook, stirring constantly, until fragrant, about 30 seconds.

4 Add the leafy green slices. Cook, stirring constantly, until bright green and slightly wilted, about 2 minutes.

5 Add the soy sauce and sesame oil. Cook, stirring constantly, until the vegetables are tender, about 1 minute. Serve right away.

VEGETABLE FRIED RICE

EQUIPMENT:

- Knife
- Cutting board
- Box grater
- Wok or large skillet
- Wooden spoon

All over Asia, people cook fried rice to use up leftover rice from the night before. Fried rice isn't really "fried," but cooked in a skillet or wok. In Southeast Asia, street vendors make fried rice to order, adding ingredients that the customer chooses.

INGREDIENTS:

3 tablespoons vegetable oil

1 onion, chopped

1 red bell pepper, chopped

1 garlic clove, minced

2 cups cooked white or brown rice

½ cup green peas

1 carrot, peeled and finely shredded

2 large eggs

3 tablespoons soy sauce

1 Heat 2 tablespoons of the oil in the wok over medium-high heat. Add the onion, pepper, and garlic. Cook, stirring constantly, until softened, about 3 minutes. ⚠ HOT

2 Add rice, peas, and carrot. Cook, stirring constantly, until vegetables are tender, about 4 minutes.

3 Push the cooked ingredients to the edge of the wok. Add the remaining 1 tablespoon oil to the center of the wok. Pour in the eggs and stir until scrambled. Slowly stir in the rice mixture until blended.

4 Add soy sauce. Cook, stirring constantly, until well blended, about 1 minute. Serve hot.

Rice

Did you know that humans eat grass? Rice is wild grass grown in fields called "paddies." A staple in Asia and the Middle East for thousands of years, rice was brought to Europe by traders in the 13th century and to the Americas in the 15th century. Most rice is white or brown, but there are red, purple, and black varieties. In Japan, sushi is made with short-grained rice. Vietnamese spring rolls contain rice noodles. A classic Middle Eastern rice dish is called *pilau*. In Italy, Arborio rice is cooked with broth to make risotto. And if someone offers you "dirty rice" in Louisiana, don't be offended! It's just been cooked with chicken livers. Rice is also used to make desserts all over the world.

Fried Rice Variations

You can make your own version of fried rice, too! Choose one of these recipes or add whatever ingredients you like. Follow the directions for Vegetable Fried Rice and add one or all of the following:

Tofu Fried Rice:
In step #4, stir in 1 cup diced firm tofu.

Meat, Chicken, or Shrimp Fried Rice:
In step #4, stir in 1 cup diced cooked meat, chicken, or shrimp.

Lemongrass Lemonade

Lemongrass is native to Southeast Asia and used in many recipes. Chop 2 lemongrass stalks. In a small saucepan, combine lemongrass, 1¾ cups water, ⅔ cup sugar, and a pinch of salt. Bring to a boil. Remove from heat and cover. Set aside for 30 minutes. Pour through a fine-mesh sieve and discard the lemongrass. Stir in ¾ cup lemon juice. Taste and add more sugar if you like. Serve over ice.

SHRIMP PAD THAI

MAKES
4
SERVINGS

EQUIPMENT:

- Knife
- Cutting board
- Fine-mesh sieve
- Medium bowls
- Wok or large skillet
- Wooden spoon

The name of this noodle dish means "stir-fried in the Thai style." It's a perfect fit: fish sauce, lime juice, chilies, and sugar are all common ingredients in Thai cooking. Pad Thai has been the national dish of Thailand since World War II, when it was made popular by Thailand's prime minister.

INGREDIENTS:

8 ounces (225 g) rice noodles

3 tablespoons soy sauce

2 tablespoons fish sauce

2 tablespoons lime juice

2 tablespoons sugar

½ teaspoon Thai red chili sauce

3 tablespoons vegetable oil

½ pound (225 g) large shrimp, peeled and deveined

1 garlic clove, minced

1½ cups bean sprouts

5 green onions, chopped

2 large eggs, broken into a small bowl and lightly beaten

To serve: chopped peanuts, chopped cilantro, lime wedges

1 In one medium bowl, cover the noodles with warm water. Soak for 10 minutes. Drain.

2 In the other bowl, whisk together ¼ cup water, soy sauce, fish sauce, lime juice, sugar, and chili sauce.

3 Heat 2 tablespoons of the oil in the wok over medium-high heat. Add the shrimp and garlic. Cook, stirring constantly, until the shrimp is just pink, about 2 minutes. ⚠ HOT

4 Push the shrimp to the edge of the skillet. Add the noodles and sauce. Using the spoon, toss the noodles until coated with sauce and push to the edge of the wok.

5 Stir in the sprouts and green onions. Push to the edge of the wok.

6 Add the remaining 1 tablespoon oil to the open area. Pour in the eggs and stir to scramble. Stir in the noodles and shrimp until mixed, about 1 minute. Serve right away.

To chop green onions: Cut off the root end, then thinly slice the white and green parts.

VIETNAMESE LETTUCE ROLLS

Lettuce rolls were created in Vietnam centuries ago. Now they are popular in Laos, Cambodia, and Thailand, too. The filling often contains chilies, and the lettuce helps cool the heat. These are less spicy than the ones in Southeast Asia, but just as tasty.

EQUIPMENT:

- Box grater
- Medium saucepan
- Fine-mesh sieve
- Cutting board

MAKES 4 SERVINGS

1 Bring 3 cups of water to a boil in the medium saucepan. Add the noodles and turn off the heat. Soak for 8 minutes. Drain in a fine-mesh sieve.

HOT

2 On the cutting board, arrange the lettuce cup-side up. Divide the noodles evenly between the cups. Pile ¼ cup chicken on top of each. Layer an equal amount of the bean sprouts, carrots, and mint leaves on top of the chicken.

3 Fold the lettuce sides over the filling. Roll up the filling in the lettuce leaf. Arrange the rolls seam side down on the work surface. Cut in half and serve immediately.

INGREDIENTS:

- 4 ounces (112 g) rice stick noodles, broken up
- 8 Bibb lettuce leaves
- 1½ cups shredded cooked chicken
- ⅔ cup bean sprouts
- ⅔ cup shredded carrots
- 16 mint leaves

To serve: Lime wedges, chopped basil leaves, and Vietnamese Dipping Sauce (see next page)

Vietnamese Dipping Sauce

This traditional dipping sauce brings out the fresh flavors of the rolls without overpowering them. In a small bowl, stir together ¼ cup fish sauce, 3 tablespoons water, 2 tablespoons lime juice, 2 tablespoons sugar, and 1 teaspoon minced garlic. Set aside until ready to serve.

PACIFIC
OCEAN

Indonesia

This country is an archipelago, which means that it's completely made up of islands. There are about 17,000 islands in all in Indonesia, but only 6,000 of them are populated! Today, Indonesia is home to more than 200 different tribes and ethnic groups. Indonesians like to add a chili sauce called *sambal oelek* to almost all their dishes. They also consume lots of fish, rice, fresh vegetables, and tropical fruits like mangoes.

I N D I A

I N D O N E S I A

India

India is home to more than one billion people, most of whom follow one of two main religions, Islam or Hinduism. Muslims do not eat pork, and Hindus do not eat beef. For this reason, many Indian dishes are vegetarian. Because India is so large, the climate varies greatly from the north to the south. The food of India is just as diverse.

INDIAN
OCEAN

AUSTRALIA

Australasia (Australia, New Zealand, and the islands northeast of Australia)

Located below the equator, this region's climate is the opposite of the northern hemisphere's: the north part of the country has warmer weather, and the south's climate is cooler. The culture and food are a mix of Aboriginal traditions and those introduced by European settlers in the 1700s. Meats like lamb, lots of fish, and tropical fruits like kiwi, mango, and coconut are all common ingredients.

NEW
ZEALAND

India, Indonesia, and Australasia

These regions all have coastlines on the Indian Ocean. They were once stops on the spice route, the path tradesmen took from Asia to the Middle East and Europe to buy and sell spices. Many English and Dutch settlers came here during the 17th and 18th centuries. Much of the food shows European influences, but uses native ingredients like mango.

The Taj Mahal, located in the north Indian city of Agra

LEMONY LAMB SKEWERS

EQUIPMENT:

- Knife
- Cutting board
- Broiler pan
- Aluminum foil
- Medium bowl
- 4 bamboo or metal skewers

Cooking foods on skewers was a way to preserve fuel as tribes moved across the outback (the vast Australian desert). Small chunks of food cook quickly, so the fire did not have to last as long. You can also cook fish or vegetables on skewers. Make sure the chunks are all about the same size so they cook evenly.

INGREDIENTS:

1 tablespoon vegetable oil

1 teaspoon finely chopped lemon zest

2 tablespoons firmly packed brown sugar

¾ teaspoon ground cumin

Salt and pepper

1½ pounds (675 g) boneless leg of lamb, cut into 16 1-inch (2.5-cm) chunks

1 lemon, cut into 8 wedges

1 green bell pepper, cut into 8 wedges

1 Arrange the oven rack in the upper third of the oven. Preheat the broiler to high. Line the broiler pan with foil.

2 In the medium bowl, stir together the oil, lemon zest, brown sugar, cumin, salt, and pepper. Add the lamb and toss the pieces to coat.

3 Working one at a time, build the skewers. Be sure to alternate the lamb with the lemon and pepper wedges. **SHARP**

4 Place the skewers on the prepared pan. Broil until the lamb pieces are well browned, 10 to 12 minutes. Using pot holders, remove the pan from the oven and serve right away. **HOT**

Skewer the thickest part of the lamb cubes so they cook more evenly.

Other Foods Down Under

Lamb is popular in Australasia, but other meats such as kangaroo and emu are commonly eaten as well. Because Australia and New Zealand are both island nations, fish is also a staple. Oysters, cod, shrimp, and a large fish called *barramundi* are all favorites.

ANZAC BISCUITS

These cookies are named for the Australian and New Zealand Army Corps (ANZAC). The nutritious coconut and oatmeal makes them a lot like energy bars—good to take on long hikes. They also are perfect for packing in lunch boxes because they don't get smashed easily. (They taste great, too!)

MAKES 24 COOKIES

EQUIPMENT:

- Cookie sheets
- Parchment paper
- Large and small bowls
- Rubber spatula
- Mini ice-cream scoop
- Wire cooling rack

INGREDIENTS:

- 1¼ cups all-purpose flour
- 1 cup old-fashioned oatmeal
- ¾ cup firmly packed light brown sugar
- ½ cup shredded coconut
- ⅓ cup chopped macadamia nuts
- 1½ teaspoons baking powder
- 6 tablespoons butter, melted
- 2 tablespoons cane sugar syrup or light corn syrup
- 1 teaspoon vanilla extract

1 Arrange the oven rack in the middle of the oven. Heat the oven to 350°F (180°C). Line two cookie sheets with parchment paper.

2 In the large bowl, stir together the flour, oatmeal, brown sugar, coconut, nuts, and baking powder.

3 In the small bowl, stir together the melted butter, syrup, 2 tablespoons warm water, and vanilla. Pour the liquid mixture over the flour mixture. Using the rubber spatula, stir until well blended.

4 Using your hands or the mini ice-cream scoop, shape the dough into 1¼-inch (3-cm) balls. Arrange the dough balls about 2 inches (5 cm) apart on the prepared cookie sheets. Press down on each ball to flatten slightly.

5 Bake one sheet at a time, until the cookies are golden brown, about 13 minutes. Using pot holders, move the cookie sheet to the cooling rack to cool completely.

⚠ HOT

PAVLOVA

EQUIPMENT:

- Cookie sheet
- Parchment paper
- Large bowl
- Electric mixer
- Rubber spatula
- Ruler

Australia and New Zealand both take credit for inventing this dessert made from meringue and fruit. It looks like a ballerina's tutu, and is actually named after Anna Pavlova, a Russian ballerina. Traditionally, "pavs" are topped with kiwi and strawberry, but you can use any fruit you like.

MAKES **6** SERVINGS

INGREDIENTS:

4 whites from large eggs
¼ teaspoon cream of tartar
1 cup sugar
2 tablespoons cornstarch
1 teaspoon white vinegar
1 teaspoon vanilla extract

1 Arrange the oven rack in the middle of the oven, and preheat to 350°F (177°C). Line the cookie sheet with parchment paper.

2 In the large bowl, combine the egg whites and cream of tartar. Beat on medium-high speed until the whites are fluffy and form soft peaks. ELECTRIC

3 With the mixer running, slowly add the sugar. Beat until firm and glossy.

4 Stop the mixer. Using the rubber spatula, scrape down the sides of the bowl. Add the cornstarch, vinegar, and vanilla. Beat until blended.

5 Using the spatula, scrape the meringue into a tall mound on the prepared sheet. Spread to form a tall 6-inch (15-cm) round with an indent in the center.

6 Place the sheet in the oven, then reduce the temperature to 200° F (93° C). Bake 1 hour 15 minutes. Turn the oven off and leave the meringue in the oven until completely cool. Serve with whipped cream and fresh fruit. HOT

Make some whipped cream for a topping or try some berries for a fresh accent.

Sweetened Whipped Cream

This is a delicious topping for all of your desserts! In a medium bowl, combine ¾ cup chilled heavy cream, 1 tablespoon sugar, and ¼ teaspoon vanilla extract. Using an electric mixer, begin beating on low speed. Gradually increase speed to high. Beat until the cream forms soft peaks when you turn off the mixer and lift the beaters. The cream can be covered and refrigerated up to 1 hour.

⚠️ ELECTRIC

TANDOORI CHICKEN LEGS

EQUIPMENT:

- Knife
- Cutting board
- Large zip-top plastic bag
- Jelly roll pan
- Aluminum foil
- Tongs

Tandoori is an Indian style of cooking that uses a marinade made from yogurt, lime or lemon juice, and spices. The yogurt and juice tenderize the meat as it cooks and also helps the spices cling to it. The spices used in tandoori-style cooking are mostly the same as those used in Indian curries.

INGREDIENTS:

- 1 container (8 ounces/250 g) plain (unflavored) yogurt
- 1 garlic clove, minced
- 1 tablespoon lemon juice
- 1 tablespoon vegetable oil
- 1½ teaspoons ground cumin
- 1½ teaspoons ground chili powder
- ½ teaspoon salt
- ¼ teaspoon ground turmeric
- 8 medium skinless whole chicken legs

To serve: chopped fresh cilantro, lime wedges, and Raita (see next page)

1 In the plastic bag, combine the yogurt, garlic, lemon juice, vegetable oil, cumin, chili powder, salt, and turmeric. Press the top of the bag so it is flat and there are no air bubbles inside and seal the bag. Gently squish the bag to mix the ingredients.

2 Carefully open the bag and add the chicken legs. Seal the bag as before and gently move the bag to coat the chicken in the yogurt mixture. Refrigerate for 4 to 8 hours.

3 Arrange the oven rack in upper third of the oven. Heat the oven to 425°F (220°C). Line the jelly roll pan with foil.

4 Using tongs, remove the chicken from the plastic bag. Leave a thick coating of the marinade on each leg. Arrange the chicken on the prepared pan. Throw away the bag and the remaining marinade.

5 Bake until the chicken is browned ⚠ HOT and cooked through, about 35 minutes. Using pot holders, remove the pan from the oven. Serve hot.

Squish the yogurt mixture between your hands until it is a consistent yellow color.

What Is a Tandoor?

Tandoori-style dishes are cooked in a special oven called a *tandoor*. Tandoors are often round like barrels with domed lids. They are made from clay, which absorbs heat and doesn't burn, so the oven stays hot for a long time. A fire is built in the bottom of the oven and the walls absorb the fire's heat. The temperature inside can be as high as 800°F (427°C), but is usually around 500°F (260°C). Food is put on long skewers and held just above the fire. The oven is so hot that meat cooks very quickly and stays juicy and flavorful. Breads like naan and roti are also cooked in a tandoor. Dough is rolled flat and slapped directly on the oven wall to bake. Because of the intense heat, the dough sticks and cooks there.

Raita

A raita is a cold yogurt sauce that is often served with spicy Indian foods. Combine 1 cup plain (unflavored) yogurt, ½ teaspoon ground cumin, and ¼ teaspoon salt in a small bowl. Add ½ cup peeled, seeded, and finely chopped cucumber, and 1 tablespoon finely chopped fresh cilantro. Cover and refrigerate until ready to serve.

CAULIFLOWER AND PEA CURRY

Curries are found all over India and Indonesia. In the north, dairy products like yogurt and a cheese called *paneer* are common ingredients. In southern India and Indonesia, curries are spicier and made with coconut milk. Indonesian curries also contain peanuts and fish paste. This dish is an example of a south Indian curry.

EQUIPMENT:

- Knife
- Cutting board
- Large skillet with a lid
- Wooden spoon

MAKES 4 SERVINGS

1 In the large skillet over medium heat, heat the oil. Add the cauliflower, garlic, and curry powder. Cook, stirring constantly, until the cauliflower is coated with the curry powder, about 2 minutes. **HOT**

2 Add the coconut milk, 1/3 cup water, and bay leaf. Stir until blended. Bring to a boil. Cover with the lid. Reduce heat to low and cook 15 minutes.

3 Using pot holders, carefully remove the lid. Stir in the peas. Replace the lid and cook until the cauliflower is tender, 5 to 8 minutes. Uncover, stir in the cilantro, and serve.

INGREDIENTS:

2 tablespoons vegetable oil

1 pound (450 g) cauliflower florets

1 garlic clove, minced

1 tablespoon curry powder

1/2 cup coconut milk

1 small bay leaf, broken into 3 pieces

1 cup frozen peas

1/4 cup chopped fresh cilantro

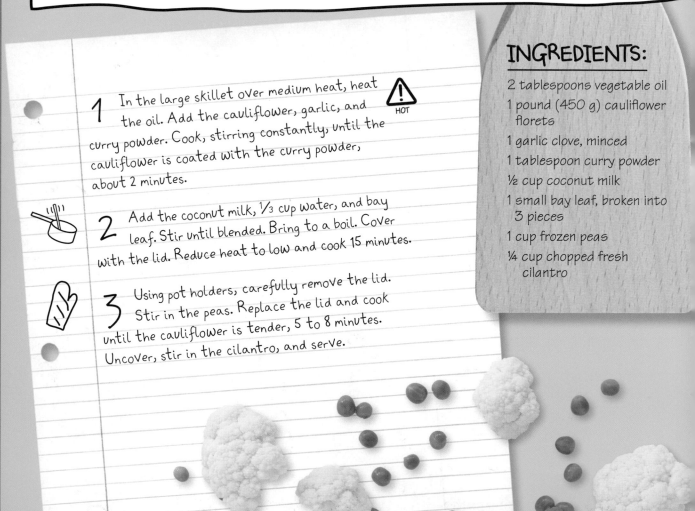

Spice Mixes

Many cultures cook with spice mixes. Curry powder is a mix of spices created by British settlers in India. Indians season food with *garam masala*. In the Middle East and Africa, *za'atar* and *ras el hanout* are widely used. French recipes often include an herb mix called *fines herbes*. In China, flavor is added with five-spice powder. In the southwest United States and Latin America, you'll usually find chili powder on the spice shelf.

Samoan Papaya Pudding

In the Pacific island of Samoa, papaya pudding is often served for breakfast. Cut 2 ripe papayas in half. Scoop out the seeds. Scoop the flesh into a blender. Add 1 ripe, peeled banana, ½ cup coconut milk, and ¼ teaspoon vanilla extract. Cover and blend until smooth, about 1 minute. To serve, pour into a bowl and sprinkle with shredded coconut.

⚠ ELECTRIC

Pocket Food Around the World

Travel around the world and you'll discover that each country has its own version of a small stuffed pastry that is eaten as a meal. They are known as "pocket foods," because the fillings are stuffed into "pockets" of dough. Pocket foods are sold by street vendors and cooked at home. They are served as snacks, appetizers, or meals.

UNITED STATES

Turnovers are made with puff pastry or pie dough and filled—usually with apples, but sometimes with cherries, blueberries, or other fruits. They make a sweet dessert or breakfast.

People in El Salvador have eaten **pupusas** for thousands of years. There's even an official to celebrate them!

Latin American specialties **tamales, humitas,** and **hallacas** are all steamed in banana leaves or corn husks.

APPLE TURNOVERS

Nonstick cooking spray
1 sheet puff pastry
2 apples
2 tablespoons sugar
½ teaspoon cinnamon
1 tablespoon milk

1. Preheat oven to 400°F (200°C). Cut the puff pastry into 4 pieces.

2. Peel and core the apples and have an adult slice them very thin. Put the apples in a bowl and add the sugar and cinnamon. Mix well until every slice is coated.

3. Place ½ cup of the apple mixture into the center of each pastry square. Fold in each corner to close the squares.

4. Brush the edges with a little milk and press down with a fork to seal.

5. Bake until golden-brown, about 12 minutes. Remove the pan from the oven and place on a wire rack. Let cool 10 minutes before serving.

LATIN AMERICA

Empanadas (from the Spanish empanar, "to wrap in bread") are eaten all over Latin America. Each country has its own version. They can be filled with meat, cheese, fish, or fruit.

Pasties were originally filled with hearty beef, potato, and onion to feed underground miners at lunchtime. These days, you can also find them with ham, chicken, turkey, cheese, or vegetables.

ENGLAND

Calzones are usually filled with cheese (ricotta and mozzarella), but meat and vegetables can be included, too. They're just like pizzas, except the toppings are inside the dough instead of on top.

ITALY

Japanese **gyoza** (dumplings filled with pork, shrimp, or cabbage) are dipped in a soy sauce–vinegar mixture.

Mandu are Korean dumplings served on the first day of the year. They are filled with fish or ground meat, vegetables, and sometimes cellophane noodles. They are fried, steamed, or simmered in broth.

KOREA

The shape of the puff pastry tells you what's inside a **boureka**: Potato filling in box-shaped bourekas, cheese in triangles; or spinach in a knot.

ISRAEL

Tunisian **brik** are made with phyllo dough wrapped around a filling of ground beef, chicken, or tuna. They may also be made with a whole egg in the middle.

TUNISIA

Filipino **empanadas** are pastries filled with meat, potatoes, and onion, then deep-fried or baked.

Meat pies are hand-size pastries filled with minced beef or chicken, onions, spices, and a thick gravy. Topped with tomato sauce, they are a favorite Aussie snack.

AUSTRALIA

The Middle East, Africa, and the Mediterranean

Southern Europe, North Africa, and the Middle East all have coastlines on the Mediterranean Sea. This region enjoys a sunny climate nearly all year long, so vegetables and herbs grow well here and are widely used in cooking. Continental Africa is also sunny and warm all year, but the diversity of the cultures means that the foods are vastly different, too.

A camel caravan crossing the Sahara desert in Africa

France

France has long been considered the culinary capital of the world, and its food is as diverse as its history. In the northern regions of Alsace and Burgundy, choucroute and coq au vin will warm you up. In the south, eggplant and tomatoes are widely grown and used in classic Provençal dishes such as ratatouille.

Greece

Greece has one of the longest coastlines in the world, and includes more than 2,000 islands. Olives, olive oil, and feta cheese are among the most well-known Greek foods. Many Greek dishes also use a paper-thin pastry called *phyllo*. Lamb is commonly eaten and is often roasted or grilled.

Spain

Spain is famous for a style of food called *tapas*, which includes small dishes like a bowl of olives, garlicky shrimp, Serrano ham with melon, spicy sausage, or Manchego cheese. Small serving sizes mean you get to try many of Spain's signature flavors in a single meal.

FRANCE

SPAIN   ITALY

GREECE

MEDITERRANEAN SEA

MOROCCO

TUNISIA

MIDDLE EAST

PERSIAN GULF

RED SEA

AFRICA

INDIAN OCEAN

ATLANTIC OCEAN

Africa

Africa is a very large continent made up of many different countries. African food is mostly made up of starchy vegetables like plantains and yams. North African food is much like Middle Eastern food. Further south, coastal countries like Nigeria use fish in their cooking. Inland countries like Botswana use more meat. Many countries, like Cameroon and South Africa, were settled by Europeans who had a big influence on the food there.

Middle East

The region known as the Middle East is made up of several countries. Many cultures have called this area home for centuries. The area is mostly desert broken up by bodies of water such as the Persian Gulf and the Red Sea. Olives, dates, chickpeas, and figs grow well here and are widely used in recipes. Nomadic cultures have had an influence on the food, which you can see in dishes like kebabs and tabbouleh.

Italy

Italy is the home of pizza, pasta, and famous cheeses. Mozzarella, ricotta, and Parmigiano Reggiano are just a few. Italy's cuisine changes in different parts of the country. In northern Italy you'll see dishes that use lots of meat and game. In the south, you'll find more recipes with tomato sauces and olive oil.

SOUTH AFRICA

FLOURLESS CHOCOLATE CAKES

Jewish people around the world celebrate the Israelites' escape from ancient Egypt during the Passover holiday. According to the story, they did not have time to wait for their bread to rise before the journey. Eating foods without flour or leavening (ingredients that make bread rise) is one way to observe the holiday.

EQUIPMENT:

- Foil cupcake liners
- 12-cup muffin pan
- Medium saucepan
- Whisk
- Toothpick
- Wire cooling rack

MAKES 12 CAKES

INGREDIENTS:

Nonstick cooking spray

1½ cups semisweet chocolate chips

8 tablespoons butter, cut into 6 pieces

⅓ cup sugar

1 teaspoon vanilla extract

3 large eggs

1 Arrange the oven rack in the middle of the oven and preheat the oven to 300°F (149°C). Put foil liners into muffin pan. Lightly spray with nonstick cooking spray.

2 In a medium saucepan, combine chocolate, ¾ cup water, and butter. Cook over low heat, stirring constantly, until melted and smooth. Remove the pan from the heat. Let cool 10 minutes. **HOT**

3 Add the sugar and vanilla to the cooled chocolate mixture. Whisk until blended. Add eggs, whisking in one egg at a time.

4 Pour the batter in to the cupcake cups, filling each cup almost to the top of the foil. Bake until a toothpick inserted into the center of a cake comes out with wet clumps on it, about 35 minutes. Using pot holders, move the pan to the cooling rack. Let cool completely. (The centers of the cakes will sink in slightly.)

5 Refrigerate the cakes in the pan until cold, about 4 hours or up to 3 days. Serve cool.

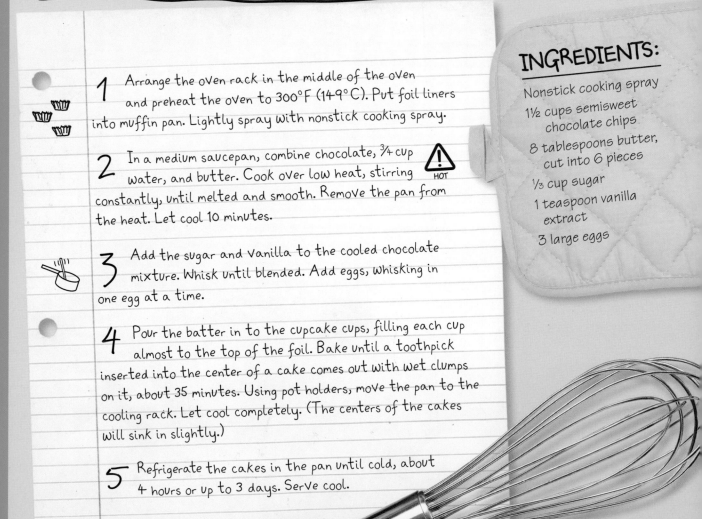

Passover

The Passover meal, called a *seder,* is a retelling of the Israelites' escape from Egypt. While the story is told, traditional prayers are recited and songs are sung. The seder can take several hours and is full of symbolic food references. A few of the symbolic foods are eaten while others are displayed on a decorated plate on the table.

TABBOULEH

Tabbouleh is a Middle Eastern salad made with lots of fresh herbs, lemon, and tomato. The recipe varies from country to country (and from family to family), using different herbs and amounts of each ingredient. It is often served with lettuce leaves, which are used to scoop up the mixture.

EQUIPMENT:

- Knife
- Cutting board
- Large bowl
- Food processor
- Fine-mesh sieve
- Wooden spoon

MAKES 4 SERVINGS

INGREDIENTS:

½ cup bulgur

1½ cups lightly packed parsley leaves

4 green onions, trimmed and cut into 2-inch (5-cm) piec

1 garlic clove

1 tablespoon lemon juice

¼ cup olive oil

10 small cherry tomatoes, cut in half

Salt and pepper

1 Put the bulgur in the large bowl. Add hot (not boiling) water to cover the bulgur. Set aside for 20 minutes. ⚠ HOT

2 Put the parsley, green onions, and garlic in the food processor. Process until finely chopped. ⚠ ELECTRIC

3 Set the sieve in the sink. Spoon the soaked bulgur into the sieve. Using the back of the wooden spoon, press on the bulgur to squeeze out all of the water.

4 In the large bowl, combine the bulgur with the parsley mixture and the lemon juice, olive oil, and tomatoes. Using the large spoon, toss until well mixed. Season with salt and pepper. Serve right away or cover and refrigerate up to 2 days.

Use the back of the spoon to press the bulgur against the side of the sieve.

Middle Eastern Food

Tabbouleh is made across the entire Middle East and Mediterranean. Here are some other staples you'll find throughout the Middle Eastern region:

• Tahini, a paste made from sesame seeds, has a variety of uses. It can be mixed with lemon juice and used as a sauce, or sweetened and made into a candy called *halvah*.

• Baba ghanoush is a dip made from roasted eggplant, olive oil, and lemon juice.

• *Hummus* is the Arabic word for chickpea. It also means a dip made from chickpeas, olive oil, lemon juice, and tahini.

• Falafel are patties made from chickpeas and herbs. They are usually fried and served in a pita pocket with lettuce, tomato, onions, and tahini.

GREEK PORK KEBABS

EQUIPMENT:

- Knife
- Cutting board
- Broiler pan
- Aluminum foil
- Medium bowl
- Spoon
- 4 bamboo or metal skewers

Just like in the outback, this fuel-efficient cooking style was a favorite of nomadic tribes in the Mediterranean and Middle East. Oregano and tomatoes are a classic Greek flavor combination. These kebabs go very well with a classic Greek salad (cucumbers, feta cheese, olives, tomatoes, and onions) and warm pita bread.

INGREDIENTS:

1 tablespoon olive oil

1 garlic clove, minced

2 teaspoons chopped fresh oregano leaves

Salt and pepper

1½ pounds (675 g) pork tenderloin, cut into 16 1-inch (2.5-cm) cubes

1 green bell pepper, cut into 8 wedges

8 large cherry tomatoes

1 Arrange the oven rack in the upper quarter of the oven and heat the broiler to high. Line the broiler pan with foil.

2 In the medium bowl, stir together the oil, garlic, and oregano. Season with salt and pepper. Add the pork and stir to coat the pieces.

3 Build the kebabs one at a time. Start with a pork cube, then a pepper piece. Add a second pork cube, then a tomato. Repeat so each skewer contains 4 pork cubes, 2 pepper wedges, and 2 tomatoes. Be sure the skewers go through the centers of the ingredients. ⚠ SHARP

4 Place the kebabs on the prepared pan. Broil, turning halfway through cooking, until browned, 10 to 12 minutes. Using pot holders, remove the pan from the oven and serve right away. ⚠ HOT

Olives

Olives have been grown in the Mediterranean and Middle East for centuries. They are too bitter to be eaten fresh. They must be cured, or preserved, in oil, water, or salt. Water- and oil-cured olives are shiny and smooth, while salt-cured olives have a wrinkled texture. Here's a small sampling of olive varieties:

• Green olives that have been stuffed with a red pimiento are Manzanilla olives from Spain.

• Gaeta olives are brine-cured olives from Spain.

• French olives include Picholine, a small green olive, and Niçoise, a small black olive.

• Kalamata is one type of Greek brine-cured black olive.

• Moroccan olives are usually salt-cured. There are hundreds of varieties.

MARINARA SAUCE

MAKES
6
SERVINGS

EQUIPMENT:

- Knife
- Cutting board
- Large pot
- Wooden spoon

Marinara means "the sauce of the sailors." It was served to sailors on Italian ships, because it is simple to make and keeps better than sauces made with meat. Serve this sauce over a bowl of freshly cooked pasta (see box) and Meatballs (see recipe, page 85).

INGREDIENTS:

3 tablespoons olive oil

1 large onion, chopped

3 garlic cloves, minced

½ teaspoon dried oregano

1 (29-ounce) can diced tomatoes in juice (not drained)

1 (29-ounce) can tomato puree

2 tablespoons sugar

1 small bay leaf

Salt and pepper

To serve: hot pasta

1 Add the oil to the pot and heat over medium heat. Add the onion. Cook, stirring frequently with the spoon, until tender and the edges are brown, about 7 minutes. ⚠ HOT

2 Add the garlic and oregano. Cook 1 minute.

3 Add the tomatoes, puree, sugar, and bay leaf. Season with salt and pepper. Bring to a boil, stirring frequently. Reduce the heat to low. Simmer, stirring occasionally, until the sauce is thick, about 20 minutes. Serve over hot pasta.

Al Dente Pasta

Al dente means "to the tooth" in Italian, so pasta cooked this way has a little bite. Fill a large pot with 4 quarts of water. Bring to a boil over high heat. Add 2 tablespoons of salt. Add 1 pound (450 g) of pasta and stir to separate the pasta. (Stir occasionally during cooking.) Cooking time depends on the type of pasta—see the package for specific times. Check your pasta about 1 minute before the shorter cooking time on the package. Using a spoon, carefully scoop out a piece of pasta and bite into it. It should be a little chewy, but not tough. When the pasta is ready, place a colander in the sink. Have an adult help you pour the pasta and water into the colander. Shake the colander until the water is drained. Serve immediately. HOT

Variations

Marinara can be the base for other classic Italian pasta sauces.

Puttanesca:
Make a batch of Marinara Sauce and add ½ cup chopped pitted black olives, 3 tablespoons drained capers, 2 mashed anchovy fillets, ⅓ cup chopped fresh parsley, and a pinch of red pepper flakes.

Pink Sauce:
Make a batch of Marinara Sauce and add 2 cups heavy cream. Cook until thickened, about 10 minutes.

Balsamic Vinegar

Balsamic is a dark-colored, sweet Italian vinegar invented in Modena, Italy, during the Middle Ages. Sweet grapes are boiled into thick syrup, then mixed with an older batch of vinegar called a "mother." The mixture is put in a series of barrels made from different types of wood. Balsamic is aged in these barrels for 3 to 12 years, or even longer. The longer it ages, the darker, thicker, and sweeter it becomes.

CAPRESE SALAD

Caprese salad originated on the Mediterranean island of Capri, off the coast of Italy. No wonder it's such a perfect dish for a summery outdoor meal. And with red tomatoes, white mozzarella, and green basil leaves, it's the colors of the Italian flag!

MAKES
4
SERVINGS

EQUIPMENT:

- Knife
- Cutting board
- Small bowl
- Whisk

1 **Make the dressing:** In the small bowl, whisk together the vinegar, garlic, and mustard. Whisking constantly, add the oil to the bowl in a very slow, steady stream. Keep whisking until vinaigrette is smooth and well blended. Stir in chives. Season with salt and pepper.

2 **Make the salad:** Stack the slices of mozzarella and tomatoes on plates. Drizzle each stack with 1 or 2 tablespoons of the vinaigrette and sprinkle with chopped basil. Serve right away.

INGREDIENTS:

3 tablespoons balsamic vinegar

1 garlic clove, minced

2 teaspoons Dijon mustard

¾ cup olive oil

1 tablespoon chopped fresh chives

Salt and pepper

1 pound (450 g) fresh mozzarella cheese, cut into ½-inch (1.25-cm)–thick slices

1 pound (450 g) mixed ripe yellow and red tomatoes, cut into ½-inch (1.25-cm)–thick slices

¼ cup chopped fresh basil

Add the oil to the vinegar as you whisk. Ask for help—this may take three hands!

VANILLA PANNA COTTA

MAKES
6
SERVINGS

EQUIPMENT:

- Small saucepan
- Wooden spoon
- Blender
- 6 custard cups or small ramekins
- Plastic wrap

In Italian, *panna cotta* means "cooked cream," but this classic Italian dessert isn't really cooked. Instead, it's thickened with gelatin and chilled so it holds its shape. This version is made with milk and ricotta, a soft Italian cheese.

INGREDIENTS:

2½ cups milk

4 teaspoons unflavored powdered gelatin

⅔ cup sugar

1 cup part-skim ricotta cheese

1 teaspoon vanilla extract

Mint leaves, for garnish

1 Pour 1 cup of the milk into the small saucepan. Sprinkle the gelatin over the milk. Let sit until the gelatin is moist and puffy, about 4 minutes. Cook over medium-low heat, stirring constantly, until the gelatin is dissolved. Don't let the mixture boil. Remove the pan from the heat and set aside.

⚠ HOT

2 In the blender, combine remaining milk, sugar, ricotta, and vanilla. Process until smooth, about 1 minute. Add the gelatin mixture. Process until blended, about 30 seconds.

⚠ ELECTRIC

3 Pour the mixture into the custard cups or ramekins. Cover with plastic wrap. Refrigerate until firm, about 6 hours. Serve cold, garnished with mint leaves.

Blueberries, raspberries, chocolate shavings, and mint make great garnishes.

Melon Granita

This icy Italian treat is super-easy to make! Set a 9 x 13-inch (22.5 x 32.5-cm) baking dish in the freezer. Cut 1 cantaloupe in half and scoop out the seeds. Scoop the flesh into a food processor. Add ¼ cup sugar, 2 tablespoons water, 1 tablespoon lemon juice, and a pinch of salt. Process until smooth. Pour the mixture into the baking dish and freeze. Every 30 minutes, scrape the surface with a fork. Freeze and scrape until the ice crystals are loose and frozen, about 2 hours.

ELECTRIC

LEB LEBI

EQUIPMENT:

- Knife
- Cutting board
- Colander
- Large saucepan with a lid
- Wooden spoon

Soup for breakfast? That's when Tunisians serve this flavorful broth-based soup. And it's not just Tunisia! In Japan, people eat miso soup (see page 24) for breakfast. In Vietnam, *pho* (noodle soup) is often served in the morning. If you order breakfast in Indonesia, you might get *lontong sayur*, a rice cake with vegetable–coconut milk soup.

INGREDIENTS:

1 (29-ounce) can chickpeas
2 tablespoons olive oil
1 large onion, chopped
¾ teaspoon caraway seeds
¼ teaspoon ground cumin
5 cups chicken or vegetable broth
1 bay leaf
Salt and pepper

1 Dump the chickpeas into a colander. Rinse and drain.

2 In the large saucepan, heat the oil over medium heat. Add the onion. Cook, stirring frequently, until soft and light brown around the edges, about 5 minutes. **HOT**

3 Add the caraway seeds and cumin. Cook, stirring, about 1 minute.

4 Stir in the chickpeas, broth, and bay leaf. Bring to a boil. Reduce heat to low and cover with the lid. Simmer until the chickpeas are very tender, about 25 minutes. Remove from the heat.

5 Using the back of the spoon, crush some of the chickpeas against the side of the pot. Season with salt and pepper. Serve warm in bowls.

More smashed chickpeas makes for thicker soup. So smash away if you like!

Hummus

Chickpeas are also the main ingredient of this delicious and simple spread, which is a favorite in the Middle East: Rinse and drain 1 (29-ounce) can chickpeas. Put in a food processor with 3 tablespoons lemon juice, ¼ cup tahini (sesame paste), ¼ cup water, 1 garlic clove, ½ teaspoon ground cumin, and ½ teaspoon salt. Process until smooth. Scrape into bowl. Serve with toasted pita crisps or fresh vegetables.

ELECTRIC

BOBOTIE

MAKES
4
SERVINGS

EQUIPMENT:

- Knife
- Cutting board
- Zester
- Medium bowl
- 8-inch (20-cm) baking dish
- Large skillet
- Fork

The original bobotie was similar to English Shepherd's Pie (see page 88). Dutch settlers brought it to South Africa in the 1650s, when the colony was used as a supply stop for Dutch trading ships. Malay slaves on the ships added spices from their homeland, creating the bobotie found in South Africa today.

INGREDIENTS:

2 slices white bread

2 cups milk

2 tablespoons vegetable oil, plus more for the baking dish

1 pound (450 g) ground turkey

1 large onion, chopped

2 teaspoons curry powder

½ cup seedless raisins

3 tablespoons mango chutney

1 teaspoon finely chopped lemon zest

Salt and pepper

2 large eggs

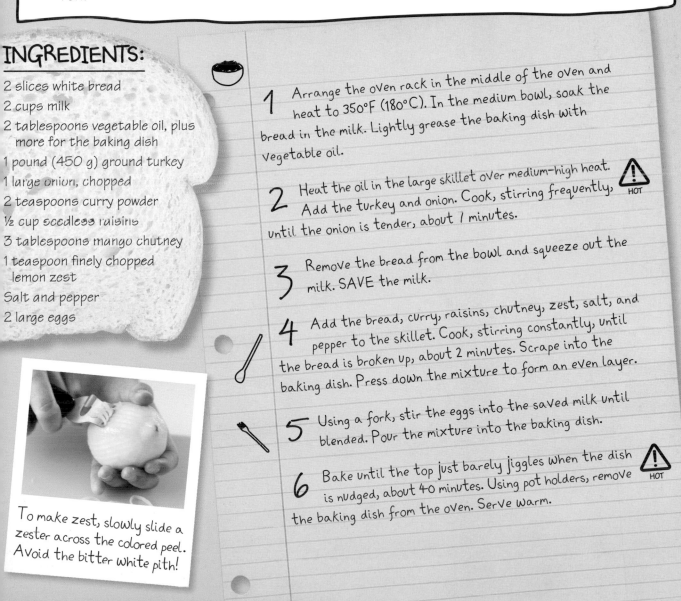

To make zest, slowly slide a zester across the colored peel. Avoid the bitter white pith!

1   Arrange the oven rack in the middle of the oven and heat to 350°F (180°C). In the medium bowl, soak the bread in the milk. Lightly grease the baking dish with vegetable oil.

2   Heat the oil in the large skillet over medium-high heat. Add the turkey and onion. Cook, stirring frequently, until the onion is tender, about 7 minutes.   ⚠️ HOT

3   Remove the bread from the bowl and squeeze out the milk. SAVE the milk.

4   Add the bread, curry, raisins, chutney, zest, salt, and pepper to the skillet. Cook, stirring constantly, until the bread is broken up, about 2 minutes. Scrape into the baking dish. Press down the mixture to form an even layer.

5   Using a fork, stir the eggs into the saved milk until blended. Pour the mixture into the baking dish.

6   Bake until the top just barely jiggles when the dish is nudged, about 40 minutes. Using pot holders, remove the baking dish from the oven. Serve warm.   ⚠️ HOT

GAZPACHO

EQUIPMENT:

- Vegetable peeler
- Knife
- Cutting board
- Food processor or blender
- Rubber spatula
- Large bowl

MAKES 4 SERVINGS

The original Arabic gazpacho contained only bread, garlic, vinegar, and olive oil. The Spanish added tomatoes (which they learned about from the Aztecs) and almonds. Eventually cucumbers and peppers were added too. This refreshing dish is often served in the hot summer months.

INGREDIENTS:

1 medium cucumber, peeled

2 pounds (900 g) ripe tomatoes, seeded and chopped

1 small onion, chopped

1 yellow pepper, chopped

2 garlic cloves, minced

3 tablespoons olive oil

2 cups tomato juice

1 tablespoon balsamic vinegar

3 tablespoons chopped fresh basil

Salt and pepper

1 Using a knife, cut the cucumber in half lengthwise. Scrape out the seeds with a small spoon. Chop the cucumber into small pieces. Set aside. **SHARP**

2 In the food processor, add the tomatoes and onion. Process until tomatoes are coarsely chopped, about 15 seconds. **ELECTRIC**

3 Add the pepper, garlic, and oil. Process until pepper is chopped into small pieces, about 15 seconds. Using the rubber spatula, scrape the ingredients into the large bowl.

4 Add the diced cucumber, tomato juice, vinegar, and basil. Season with salt and pepper. Stir with the spatula until well blended. Cover and refrigerate until very cold, about 3 hours.

5 Serve very cold with fresh basil or another garnish.

Crisp croutons, chopped black olives, sour cream, and fresh basil make perfect toppings.

RATATOUILLE

EQUIPMENT:

- Knife
- Cutting board
- Large skillet
- Wooden spoon

Ratatouille is a vegetable stew that comes from the region of France called Provence (pro-VAHNTS). Its name comes from the French word *touiller*, which means "to stir." Once you've made it, you'll understand why!

INGREDIENTS:

1 small eggplant

1 medium zucchini

4 tablespoons olive oil

1 yellow bell pepper, chopped

6 green onions, cut into 1-inch (2.5-cm) pieces

1 garlic clove, minced

1 teaspoon fresh thyme leaves

18 cherry tomatoes, cut in half

1 tablespoon balsamic vinegar

Salt and pepper

1 Trim off both ends of the eggplant and cut into 1-inch (2.5-cm) chunks. SHARP

2 Trim off both ends of the zucchini. Cut into ½-inch (1.25-cm)—thick slices.

3 Heat the oil in a large skillet over medium heat. Add the eggplant and peppers. Cook, stirring frequently, until almost tender, about 8 minutes. HOT

4 Add the zucchini, green onions, garlic, and thyme. Cook, stirring frequently, until all the vegetables are tender, about 5 minutes.

5 Add the tomatoes and vinegar. Season with salt and pepper. Cook, stirring frequently, until the tomatoes soften, about 2 minutes. Serve hot or cold.

CROQUE MONSIEUR

A classic French Croque Monsieur (or "Mister Crunch") is a grilled ham and cheese sandwich topped with a French cream sauce called *béchamel*. You can also add sliced tomatoes or use other types of cheese like blue cheese, Brie, or cheddar.

EQUIPMENT:

- Small saucepan
- Whisk
- Large skillet
- Spatula
- Knife

MAKES
4
SERVINGS

INGREDIENTS:

6 tablespoons butter
5½ teaspoons flour
1 cup milk
1 tablespoon Dijon mustard
Pinch of ground nutmeg
Salt and pepper
8 slices sandwich bread
8 slices Gruyère cheese
8 slices baked ham

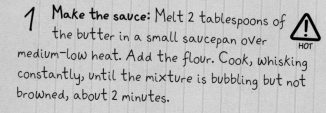

1 **Make the sauce:** Melt 2 tablespoons of the butter in a small saucepan over medium-low heat. Add the flour. Cook, whisking constantly, until the mixture is bubbling but not browned, about 2 minutes. ⚠ HOT

2 Pour in the milk. Cook, whisking constantly, until the sauce is boiling. Continue whisking and boil 2 minutes. Move the pan from the heat. Whisk in the mustard and nutmeg. Season with salt and pepper.

3 **Make the sandwiches:** Spread a bread slice with about 2 tablespoons sauce. On top of the sauce, arrange a slice of cheese, 2 slices of ham, and another slice of cheese. Spread 2 tablespoons more sauce and top with another slice of bread. Repeat to make 3 more sandwiches.

4 Melt 2 tablespoons butter in the skillet over low heat. Add 2 sandwiches. Cook until the bottoms are golden brown, about 4 minutes. Use a spatula to turn each sandwich and cook until the cheese is melted, about 4 minutes. ⚠ HOT

5 Move the sandwiches to a plate. Press down gently on each and cut in half. Repeat with remaining butter and sandwiches. Serve right away.

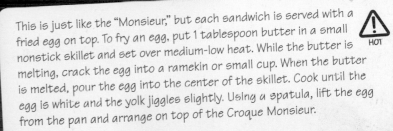

Croque Madame

This is just like the "Monsieur," but each sandwich is served with a fried egg on top. To fry an egg, put 1 tablespoon butter in a small nonstick skillet and set over medium-low heat. While the butter is melting, crack the egg into a ramekin or small cup. When the butter is melted, pour the egg into the center of the skillet. Cook until the egg is white and the yolk jiggles slightly. Using a spatula, lift the egg from the pan and arrange on top of the Croque Monsieur.

⚠ HOT

Cheese Around the World

Cheese is one of the world's oldest foods. It is made all over the world and from all kinds of milk, but mostly from the milk of cows, sheep, and goats. More exotic cheeses are made of milk from buffalo (Italy and India), camels (Middle East and Africa) and even yaks (Tibet). The cheeses on these pages hail from around the world, but you'll be able to spot most of them in your own local supermarket.

UNITED STATES

Cheddar, a firm cow's milk cheese originally from England, is now a specialty of Vermont, Wisconsin, and many other regions of the United States. Naturally a pale cream color, it's commonly tinted orange with a natural dye called annatto.

BRAZIL

Queijo coalho is a firm, salty cheese made in Brazil. It's often cut into cubes and cooked on a stick over a fire, like a kebab.

CHEESEMAKING

The milk and added flavors can vary from place to place, but the process used to make cheese is basically the same everywhere. Milk is warmed to a temperature that helps bacteria grow very quickly. Once there's enough bacteria, the cheesemaker adds an enzyme called rennet that comes from the lining of a cow's stomach. Rennet makes the milk coagulate, or clump together, into curds. The watery liquid left behind from the curdling (whey) is drained off. The cheese curds are either cut into blocks and pressed or put into molds to ripen. After the ripening (anywhere from a couple of weeks to several years), you have cheese!

Queso fresco means "fresh cheese" in Spanish. It is a pure white cow's milk cheese, with a mild, slightly salty flavor and a soft, crumbly texture.

MEXICO

Stilton is made in only three counties in England. The blue veins of mold develop during aging.

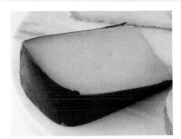

Gouda is named for a city in Holland. It's made into wheels that are dipped into red wax.

Raclette is a classic "Swiss cheese," with tiny holes and a nutty flavor. It is used to make a dish also called Raclette.

Mozzarella is traditionally made from water buffalo's milk. It is soft and slightly sweet. It's sold in different sizes, from bite-size pieces to balls bigger than your hand.

Indian **paneer** is one of the few cheeses made without rennet. It also doesn't melt when it's heated!

Brie is a very creamy cheese made from cow's milk. It has a rich, buttery flavor. Brie has been made in France for more than one thousand years.

FRANCE

Halloumi is mildly tangy and has a soft, springy texture. It can be grilled or fried without melting (it just gets softer).

GREECE

Feta is a rich and tangy cheese made all over the Middle East and Mediterranean.

United Kingdom

The United Kingdom includes England, Scotland, Wales, and Northern Ireland. Fish and chips is one of the most popular take-away meals in England, but Indian curries run a close second. Afternoon tea is a ritual that has endured over the centuries and still includes traditional favorites like tea sandwiches and scones.

Belgium

This country is considered the banking capital of the world, but that's not all there is to Belgium! Belgian chocolate is considered some of the best in the world. Waffles and *frites* (French fries to some) were both invented in Belgium.

Scandinavia (Sweden, Norway, Denmark, Finland)

The countries of Scandinavia are diverse in geography and climate. Norway is home to many fjords, or glacial inlets. Denmark is mostly flat, and Sweden is mountainous and covered with lakes. Finland is almost completely covered with forests. Reindeer, pastries, and cold-water fish like salmon are all common Scandinavian dishes.

Russia

Russia has the largest land area of any country, covering much of Asia as well as part of Europe. Because of the cold weather, many Russian dishes are stews that will warm you up. Beets, smoked fish, and sour cream are common ingredients in Russian cooking.

ARCTIC OCEAN

ICELAND

SWEDEN

FINLAND

NORWAY

RUSSIA

Ireland

The "Emerald Isle" got its name from the lush greenery that covers most of the island. Some traditional Irish dishes are boxty, colcannon, and champ, all of which use potatoes. Irish cooking also uses lots of cabbage.

DENMARK

UNITED KINGDOM

IRELAND

GERMANY

BELGIUM

ATLANTIC OCEAN

SWITZERLAND

HUNGARY

Switzerland

Switzerland borders on Germany, France, and Italy, and its culture and cuisine are influenced by those countries. Skiers love the Swiss Alps— partly because of the delicious hot chocolate offered there. Other Swiss dishes are *fondue* and *muesli,* which many Swiss eat for breakfast.

Hungary

Hungary's mix of Northern European and Turkish influences has made Hungarian culture and cooking unique. Cabbage and potatoes are widely used, often spiced with paprika, which was introduced by Turkish settlers.

Germany

Germany is a country with many characteristics, from the cutting-edge culture of the capital, Berlin, to the beautiful forests of Bavaria. Every October, millions of people visit Munich for Oktoberfest, where they eat sausages, sauerkraut, and *späetzle,* or dumplings.

Russia and Northern Europe

Rainy days, rich history, and hearty cuisine: these are features of Russia, Scandinavia, the United Kingdom, and northern continental Europe. Potatoes and root vegetables like beets are widely used in cooking. Lots of pickled fish and vegetables can be found in the northern areas. The southern countries enjoy sausages, chocolate, and pastries.

Cottages on a steep English hillside

APPLE-NUT BRUSSELS SPROUTS

Named after their place of origin, Brussels sprouts resemble tiny cabbages. They sprout from stalks that can grow up to 4 feet (1.2 m) tall. When they are roasted or sautéed, they develop a sweet, nutty flavor that the pecans and apples in this recipe really accent.

EQUIPMENT:

- Knife
- Cutting board
- Melon baller
- Large skillet
- Wooden spoon

MAKES 4 SERVINGS

1 Peel the tough outer leaves from the sprouts and cut away the bottom stems. Cut each sprout into quarters. Use the melon baller to core the apple, then chop into chunks. ⚠ SHARP

2 Melt the butter in the large skillet over medium heat. Add the onion and pecans. Cook, stirring, until the onion is soft and pecans are toasted, about 4 minutes. ⚠ HOT

3 Add the sprouts, apple, and thyme. Cook, stirring frequently, until the apples are almost tender, about 7 minutes.

4 Stir in the apple cider and balsamic vinegar. Boil 1 minute. Season with salt and pepper. Serve right away.

INGREDIENTS:

1 pound (450 g) Brussels sprouts

1 red-skinned apple

3 tablespoons butter

1 small onion, chopped

⅓ cup chopped pecans

1 teaspoon fresh thyme leaves

2 tablespoons apple cider

1 tablespoon balsamic vinegar

Salt and pepper

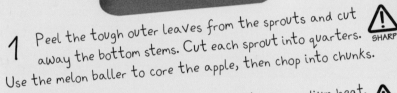

The tough outer leaves of Brussels sprouts are loose and easy to peel away.

WARM GERMAN POTATO SALAD

In Germany, potato salad is made with bacon and vinegar and served warm. In Scandinavia, you'll taste dill and sometimes sardines. In France, capers and Dijon mustard are used. Both of these versions are usually served at room temperature. In the United States, potato salad is made with either mayonnaise or yellow mustard and eaten cold.

EQUIPMENT:

- Knife
- Cutting board
- Plate
- Paper towels
- Large saucepan
- Colander
- Large skillet
- Tongs
- Wooden spoon

MAKES 4 SERVINGS

INGREDIENTS:

1 pound (450 g) small red- or white-skinned potatoes (about 9), scrubbed

Salt and pepper

5 slices bacon (about ¼ pound/112 g)

1 red bell pepper, diced

2 celery stalks, thinly sliced

1 teaspoon mustard seeds

¼ cup cider vinegar

4 green onions, trimmed and thinly sliced

1 Line a plate with a double thickness of paper towels. Put the potatoes and 1 tablespoon salt in the pan and cover with cold water. Bring to a boil over high heat. Reduce heat and simmer until potatoes are tender, about 15 minutes. Drain the potatoes. Set them aside until cool enough to handle (but still warm). Cut potatoes into quarters. **HOT** **SHARP**

2 Meanwhile, arrange the bacon slices in the skillet. Cook over medium-low heat, turning with the tongs, until golden brown, about 6 minutes. Using the tongs, remove the bacon to the paper towel-lined plate. SAVE the bacon drippings in the skillet. **HOT**

3 Add the red pepper, celery, and mustard seeds to the skillet. Cook over medium heat, stirring frequently, until the vegetables are tender, about 3 minutes.

4 Pour ¼ cup water and the vinegar into the skillet and boil for 1 minute. Remove the skillet from the heat. Stir in the potatoes and green onions. Season with salt and pepper. Serve warm.

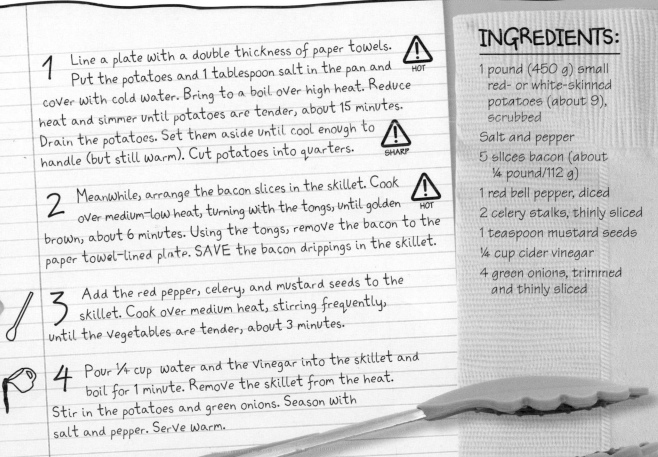

PFEFFERNÜSSE

EQUIPMENT:

- Zester
- Cookie sheets
- Parchment paper
- Medium and large bowls
- Whisk
- Electric mixer
- Mini ice-cream scoop
- Wire cooling rack
- Small sieve

Do these small, hard, peppery cookies remind you of nuts? *Pfeffernüsse* is German for "pepper-nuts." They are a traditional Christmas treat in Germany, where they are dunked in tea to make them soft enough to bite. This version is less crunchy, but still delicious dipped in tea or hot chocolate!

INGREDIENTS:

- 1¾ cup all-purpose flour
- 1 teaspoon baking powder
- 1 teaspoon ground cinnamon
- ¼ teaspoon ground nutmeg
- ½ teaspoon ground ginger
- ¼ teaspoon ground black pepper
- 8 tablespoons butter (room temperature)
- ½ cup firmly packed light brown sugar
- ¼ cup honey
- 1 large egg yolk
- 1 teaspoon finely chopped orange zest
- ½ cup confectioners' sugar

1 Preheat the oven to 350°F (180°C). Line the cookie sheets with parchment paper.

2 In a medium bowl, whisk together the flour, baking powder, cinnamon, nutmeg, ginger, and pepper.

3 In a large bowl, combine the butter and brown sugar. Beat on medium speed until well blended. ⚠ ELECTRIC

4 Add the honey, egg yolk, and zest. Mix until well blended. Add the flour mixture. Mix on low speed until blended.

5 With the ice-cream scoop, place balls of dough on the cookie sheet, leaving about 2 inches (5 cm) between each one. Press gently on each ball to flatten slightly.

6 Bake until the edges are light brown, about 14 minutes. ⚠ HOT Using pot holders, move the cookie sheet to the cooling rack. Sift confectioners' sugar over the cooled cookies.

"INSTANT" SWISS HOT CHOCOLATE

A popular wintertime activity in Switzerland is to ski in the Alps, a mountain range that runs along the Swiss border. There are cottages on the slopes for skiers to warm up a little before heading back out to the slopes. A cup of hot chocolate like this one would certainly do the trick!

EQUIPMENT:

- Blender
- Small saucepan
- Whisk

MAKES
6
SERVINGS

INGREDIENTS:

½ cup sugar

½ cup unsweetened cocoa powder

Pinch of salt

4 (1.55-ounce) bars bittersweet chocolate

¾ cup milk

Marshmallows, for serving

1 **To make the mix:** In the blender, combine sugar, unsweetened cocoa powder, and a pinch of salt. Break up the chocolate bars and add to the blender. Process until the mixture is blended and almost smooth. Transfer to an airtight container and store up to 2 months. ⚠ ELECTRIC

2 **To make a serving:** Combine 2 to 3 tablespoons mix and ¾ cup milk in the small saucepan. Whisk over low heat until the mixture is blended and the milk is steaming, about 1 minute. (Don't let the milk boil.) For an extra treat, float a few marshmallows on top. ⚠ HOT

CHICKEN PAPRIKASH

EQUIPMENT:

- Knife
- Cutting board
- Large skillet with a lid
- Tongs
- Small bowl

Csirkepaprikás, or chicken paprikash, is an example of Hungarian *goulash*, or stew. Goulash comes from the Hungarian word *gulyás*, which means "cowboy." Cowboys used to make soups and stews similar to this one over campfires while on cattle drives.

INGREDIENTS:

2 tablespoons vegetable oil

1½ pounds (675 g) boneless, skinless chicken thighs (6 thighs)

1 medium onion, chopped

1 green bell pepper, chopped

1 tablespoon sweet Hungarian paprika

1 (15-ounce) can diced tomatoes (NOT drained)

½ cup sour cream

1 tablespoon all-purpose flour

Salt and pepper

To serve: cooked egg noodles

1 In the large skillet, heat the oil over medium heat. Add the chicken and cook until browned, 4 to 5 minutes. Using tongs, turn the chicken and cook 4 or 5 minutes more, until browned. Remove from the skillet and set aside. HOT

2 Reduce the heat to medium. Add the onion and pepper to the skillet. Cook, stirring, until tender and browned at the edges, 8 to 10 minutes.

3 Sprinkle the paprika over the vegetables and cook, stirring constantly, until the veggies are coated, about 45 seconds.

4 Add the tomatoes and ½ cup water. Bring to a boil, stirring frequently, scraping up any brown bits from the skillet.

5 Add chicken and reduce the heat. Place the lid to almost cover the pot and simmer, stirring occasionally, until the chicken is cooked, 18 to 20 minutes.

6 In the small bowl, stir the sour cream and flour until smooth. When chicken is cooked, stir in the sour cream mixture. Season with salt and pepper. Boil 2 minutes, stirring, until liquid is thickened. Serve hot with egg noodles.

Paprika

Paprikash gets its name from paprika, a spice used often in Hungarian cooking. It's made from ground dried peppers, and can be rusty-orange to dark red in color. The flavor is usually mild, but gets more intense when heated. Other types of peppers, like cayenne, can be added to make paprika spicy and very hot. In addition to adding spicy flavor, paprika is sometimes sprinkled on food to give a burst of red color.

ROASTED BEETS

EQUIPMENT:

- Zester
- 9 x 13–inch (23 x 33–cm) glass baking dish (or small baking pan)
- Knife
- Cutting board
- Aluminum foil
- Vegetable brush
- Medium bowl

Root vegetables like beets and turnips are staples in the Russian diet, because they grow underground and can survive the harsh Siberian winters. They can be made into hearty soups and stews, or delicious side dishes like this one. We've added orange zest and dill to help bring out the earthy sweetness of the beets.

INGREDIENTS:

1 pound mixed red and gold medium beets

4 teaspoons vegetable oil

2 teaspoons fresh thyme leaves

Salt and pepper

2 tablespoons chopped fresh dill

1 tablespoon finely chopped orange zest

SHARP

1 Preheat the oven to 425°F (220°C). Line the bottom of the small baking dish with foil. Scrub and trim the ends of the beets, but do not peel them. Cut each beet into 1-inch (2.5-cm)—thick wedges.

2 In the bowl, combine the beet wedges, oil, and thyme. Season with salt and pepper. Toss until beets are evenly covered with oil and herbs.

3 Scrape the beets, herbs, and oil into the baking dish and spread into an even layer. Cover tightly with foil. Roast the beets for about 45 minutes or until tender.
HOT

4 Using pot holders, remove the dish from the oven. Let beets cool in the dish about 10 minutes. Carefully remove foil and sprinkle with dill and orange zest. Toss to mix and serve warm or at room temperature.

If you prefer, pinch the skins from the cooled beets before adding the dill and zest.

Roasted Beet Salad

Roasted beets are a delicious addition to salads like this one. Mix 2 cups roasted beet wedges with 3 cups mixed salad greens, ½ cup dried cranberries, ¾ cup chopped walnuts, and 4 ounces (125 g) crumbled creamy goat cheese. Drizzle with a mixture of ½ cup orange juice, 2 tablespoons olive oil, and 1 tablespoon honey.

Smorgasbord

The Swedish word *smorgasbord* is a combination of the words *smorgas* (open sandwich) and *bord* (table). It is a traditional Scandinavian celebration meal in which many foods are arranged on a large table. Guests help themselves to as many of the dishes as they like. Classic *smorgasbord* dishes are herring, smoked eel, salmon, cheeses, pickled vegetables, and Swedish meatballs.

SWEDISH MEATBALLS

EQUIPMENT:

- Knife
- Cutting board
- Large bowl
- Large skillet
- Tongs
- Plate
- Aluminum foil
- Whisk

The traditionally Swedish way to serve these meatballs is with noodles, sour cream sauce, and lingonberry jam. (Lingonberries are tart, bright red berries that grow all over Scandinavia.) This recipe can also be used to make larger meatballs to serve with spaghetti and Marinara Sauce (see page 54).

INGREDIENTS:

For the meatballs:

1 cup plain bread crumbs

¼ cup milk

1 large egg yolk

1 tablespoon Worcestershire sauce

1¼ pounds (675 g) ground beef

1 small onion, minced

¾ salt

¼ teaspoon pepper

¼ teaspoon ground nutmeg

3 tablespoons vegetable oil

For the sauce:

2 tablespoons all-purpose flour

1¾ cups beef broth

¼ cup sour cream

1 tablespoon chopped fresh dill

Salt and pepper

1 **Make the meatballs:** In a large bowl, stir the bread crumbs, milk, egg yolk, and Worcestershire sauce until blended. Add the meat, onion, salt, pepper, and nutmeg. Using your hands, gently mix until blended. Shape mixture into 36 small (or 12 large) meatballs.

2 Heat the oil in the large skillet over medium heat. Add half of the meatballs. Cook, turning, until brown on all sides, about 7 minutes. Using tongs, move meatballs to a plate. Cover with foil. Repeat with remaining meatballs.

⚠ HOT

3 **Make the sauce:** Add the flour to the skillet. Cook over medium heat, whisking, until deep brown. Whisk in the beef broth until smooth. Bring to a boil. Cook, whisking, 2 minutes.

4 Remove from the heat. Whisk in the sour cream and dill. Season with salt and pepper. Add the cooked meatballs and any juice. Stir until meatballs are covered. Serve right away.

Keep the pressure on the meatballs light—you don't want to squash them!

MASHED POTATOES

EQUIPMENT:

- Vegetable peeler
- Knife
- Cutting board
- Large saucepan
- Colander
- Potato masher

The Inca Indians of Peru were the first to grow potatoes, but people usually think of potatoes as Irish. Most of us are familiar with white or light yellow potatoes, but there are blue and purple varieties, too. We like russets for this recipe because they are light and fluffy when mashed.

INGREDIENTS:

1¼ pounds russet potatoes, peeled and cut into 1½-inch (3.75-cm) chunks

Salt and pepper

½ cup milk

3 tablespoons butter, cut into 3 pieces

Don't worry if there are lumps in your potatoes—the texture is nice!

1 Place the potatoes in the large saucepan. Add 2 teaspoons salt and enough cold water to cover them by about 1 inch (2.5 cm). Set the pan over high heat and bring to a boil. **HOT**

2 Reduce heat to medium-low and simmer until the potatoes are tender, 15 to 20 minutes. Place the colander in the sink and pour the water and potatoes into the colander to drain. **HOT**

3 Return the potatoes to the saucepan. Using the potato masher or a large fork, press down on the potatoes. Repeat until they are mashed.

4 Add the milk and butter and stir until well blended. Season with salt and pepper. Serve hot or warm.

Colcannon

Cabbage and potatoes are both Irish staples. And you can have them both in one dish! Thinly slice and chop ¼ of a small green cabbage (2½ cups). In a medium skillet, melt 1 tablespoon butter over medium heat. Add the cabbage and a pinch of salt. Cook, stirring frequently, until tender and the edges are just golden, about 10 minutes. Scrape into a batch of Mashed Potatoes and stir until combined.

SHARP

HOT

SHEPHERD'S PIE

EQUIPMENT:

- Knife
- Cutting board
- Large skillet
- Wooden spoon
- 8-inch (20-cm) glass baking dish
- Large spoon

Named for the shepherds tending their sheep around the English countryside, this one-dish meal was originally made with ground lamb. The non-lamb version is officially called "cottage" pie, but most folks still refer to it as Shepherd's Pie. "Shepherdess" pie is a vegetarian version that contains beans or lentils instead of meat.

INGREDIENTS:

1 tablespoon vegetable oil
1 pound ground turkey
1 onion, chopped
1 carrot, peeled and thinly sliced
2 tablespoons all-purpose flour
1 teaspoon fresh thyme leaves
1⅔ cups beef broth
2 tablespoons Worcestershire sauce
1 cup frozen peas
Salt and pepper
1 recipe Mashed Potatoes (see page 86)

1 Preheat the oven to 375°F (190°C).

2 Heat the oil in a large skillet over medium-high heat. Add turkey, onion, and carrot. Cook, stirring, until the meat is crumbled and the vegetables are tender, 7 to 9 minutes. HOT

3 Add the flour and thyme. Cook, stirring constantly, until the flour is light brown, about 45 seconds.

4 Add the broth, Worcestershire sauce, and peas. Season with salt and pepper. Bring to a boil, stirring frequently, scraping up any brown bits from the skillet. Boil 2 minutes, or until liquid is thickened. Pour into the baking dish.

5 Spoon an even layer of the Mashed Potatoes onto the filling. Bake until potatoes are hot and filling is bubbling around the edges, 25 to 30 minutes. Using pot holders, remove the dish from the oven. Serve hot. HOT

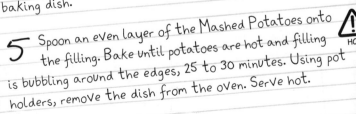

YORKSHIRE PUDDINGS

MAKES 12 PUDDINGS

EQUIPMENT:

- 12-cup muffin pan
- 2 medium bowls
- Whisk
- Wire cooling rack

This traditional English side dish was originally cooked in the hot drippings from meat roasting over an open fire. Heating the pan first makes a crisp crust form on the bottoms of the puddings. In the United States, these are called popovers because they "pop over" the edges of the cups.

INGREDIENTS:

1 cup all-purpose flour
½ teaspoon salt
1 cup milk
3 large eggs
2 tablespoons vegetable oil
1 tablespoon Dijon mustard
Nonstick cooking spray

1 Arrange the oven rack in the middle of the oven and place the muffin pan on the rack. Heat the oven to 425°F (220°C).

2 In a medium bowl, whisk together the flour and salt.

3 In a separate medium bowl, whisk together the milk, eggs, oil, and mustard. Pour the milk mixture over the flour and whisk until smooth. Set aside.

4 Using pot holders, carefully remove the muffin pan and set it on the cooling rack. Spray the insides of the muffin cups. Pour the batter evenly into the cups. Immediately return the hot pan to the oven.

⚠️ HOT

5 Keeping the oven door closed (no peeking!), bake until puffed and deep brown on top, 18 to 22 minutes. Using potholders, remove the muffin pan to the cooling rack. Serve immediately.

SCONES

EQUIPMENT:

- Zester
- Cookie sheet
- Parchment paper
- Food processor
- Large bowl
- Rubber spatula
- Small bowl
- Large ice-cream scoop
- Wire cooling rack

The name of these small, tender teacakes can be pronounced to rhyme with "own" or "on" or "moon." They are often served at high tea, along with thickened cream called clotted cream and jam or molasses. These are best when they're eaten the same day they're made.

INGREDIENTS:

2 cups all-purpose flour

½ cup sugar

2¼ teaspoons baking powder

½ teaspoon salt

8 tablespoons cold butter, cut into 10 pieces

1 teaspoon finely chopped lemon zest

¾ cup milk

1 teaspoon vanilla extract

Overmixing makes the scones tough, so be sure to mix just until the butter is pea-sized.

1 Preheat the oven to 400°F (200°C). Line the cookie sheet with parchment paper.

2 In the food processor, blend together the flour, sugar, baking powder, and salt. Scatter the cold butter over the flour. Process with short pulses until the butter is mixed in. ⚠ ELECTRIC

3 Carefully dump the butter-flour mixture into a large bowl. Using a rubber spatula, fold in the lemon zest.

4 Mix the milk and vanilla in a small bowl. Pour the milk mixture over the butter-flour mixture. Gently stir just until it forms a moist dough.

5 Using the ice-cream scoop, place eight equal-size mounds of dough about 2 inches (5 cm) apart on the cookie sheet.

6 Bake until puffed and golden brown, about 18 to 20 minutes. Using pot holders, move the cookie sheet to the cooling rack. Serve warm or at room temperature. HOT

Afternoon Tea

In England in the 1700s, only two meals—breakfast and a late dinner—were served each day. Afternoon tea began as a way to stave off hunger until dinner. Afternoon tea, or "low" tea (because it was served on a low tea table), is not just a pot of tea. There are sandwiches (cucumber is traditional) and pastries (scones or crumpets) served with preserves and clotted cream. Low tea is often followed by a sweet (like a trifle or cookies). High tea is served later in the afternoon (and on a higher table). It's a bigger meal with meats and fish served along with the other goodies.

South America, Mexico, and the Caribbean

Sunny beaches, jagged mountains, dense forests, and arid deserts can all be found in this part of the world. Most of this region also shares a warm climate, an abundance of tropical fruit, and a love of spicy foods. Corn-based dishes like tortillas and tamales are favorites, as are spicy sauces like salsa and chimichurri.

Sundrenched Mayan ruins on the eastern coast of Mexico

MEXICO

GULF OF
MEXICO

CUBA

JAMAICA   DOMINICAN
REPUBLIC

Caribbean Islands

Located to the north of South America, this area is made up of more than 7,000 islands. Almost all of the islands are surrounded by the Caribbean Sea. Fish and shellfish are commonly used here, often cooked just minutes after being pulled from the ocean. Curries are made from recipes passed down through generations of ex-slaves brought over from Africa by European settlers. Because of their lush surroundings, warm weather, and clear blue oceans, these islands are popular vacation spots.

CARIBBEAN SEA

Mexico

Mexico is the fifth largest country in the Americas and the fourteenth largest in the world. Sandwiched between the Pacific Ocean and the Gulf of Mexico, this North American country enjoys a climate that is warm and mostly tropical. Mexico is known for its Aztec and Mayan ruins, beautiful beaches, and spicy food.

PERU

SOUTH
AMERICA

PACIFIC
OCEAN

South America

South America is home to many countries and climates because the northern part lies on the equator and the southern tip is near the Antarctic Circle. You'll find the Amazon rain forest, the Amazon River, the Andes Mountains, and the Atacama Desert here. Beef from South America's many cattle ranches is a mainstay of the region's cooking. Potatoes are native to South America and are a favorite ingredient, too. South American food also has influences from both European settlers and African slaves.

ARGENTINA

ATLANTIC
OCEAN

BURGERS WITH CHIMICHURRI

An American classic—the hamburger—has a South American flavor when topped with chimichurri. This thick sauce is made from herbs, much like Italian *pesto*. In Argentina, chimichurri is served on the side with everything, like ketchup in the United States, or *kim chee* in Korea.

EQUIPMENT:

- Food processor or blender
- Small bowl
- Medium bowl
- Large skillet
- Spatula

MAKES 4 SERVINGS

INGREDIENTS:

For the chimichurri:
¾ cup packed fresh parsley
¾ cup packed fresh cilantro
¼ cup vegetable oil
1 garlic clove
2 tablespoons lemon juice
½ teaspoon ground cumin
1 teaspoon salt
¼ teaspoon pepper

For the burgers:
1 pound (450 g) ground beef
½ teaspoon ground cumin
Salt and pepper
2 tablespoons vegetable oil

To serve: lettuce, tomato, onion, and pita bread

1 **Make the chimichurri:** Put parsley, cilantro, oil, garlic, lemon juice, cumin, salt, and pepper in a food processor or blender. Process until blended and the herbs are finely chopped, about 1 minute. Pour into a small bowl and refrigerate.  ⚠ ELECTRIC

2 **Make the burgers:** Put the ground beef into the medium bowl and sprinkle with the cumin. Season with salt and pepper. Using your hands, gently mix just until combined.

3 Divide the mixture into 4 equal portions. Shape each piece into a 4-inch (10-cm) patty.

4 Heat the oil in the skillet over medium-high heat. Carefully add the patties and cook until browned on the bottom, about 3 minutes. ⚠ HOT

5 Using the spatula, carefully turn the patties and cook until browned and cooked through, 5 to 6 minutes. Remove the burgers from the skillet. Drizzle the burgers with Chimichurri Sauce and serve with lettuce, tomato, red onion, and pita bread.

Churrascaria

Churrascarias are very popular Argentinean steakhouse restaurants. The name comes from *churrasco,* which is meat cooked over a fire in an open pit. At a churrascaria, the food is served *rodizio*-style—the waiters "rotate" between the tables, carrying meat on long skewers. When you are ready for your next helping, the waiter cuts off pieces of meat and puts them on your plate. But be sure to tell them when to stop, or you may get more than you bargained for!

Sweet Potatoes Around the World

Add international flavor to your next batch of spuds with one of these variations:

Indian:
1½ teaspoons curry powder

Hungarian:
2 tablespoons brown sugar
1½ teaspoons Hungarian paprika

Caribbean:
1 tablespoon brown sugar
1 teaspoon ground cumin
½ teaspoon ground cinnamon
Pinch of allspice

ROASTED SWEET POTATO FRIES

Potatoes are *tubers*, or vegetables that grow underground. Native to South America, they grow in colors ranging from white to orange to yellow—even purple. Roasting is an easy way to cook all potatoes, but roasted sweet potatoes are especially tasty.

EQUIPMENT:

- Vegetable brush
- Large jelly roll pan
- Aluminum foil
- Knife
- Cutting board

MAKES
4
SERVINGS

INGREDIENTS:

3 medium sweet potatoes, scrubbed and dried
2 tablespoons vegetable oil
Coarse salt
Pepper

1 Arrange the oven rack in the upper third of the oven and heat the oven to 450° F (230°C). Line a jelly roll pan with foil.

2 Using a knife, cut each potato in half lengthwise. Cut each half into 3 long wedges. Place the wedges in a large bowl. ⚠ SHARP

3 Add the oil, salt, and pepper, and any additional ingredients (see box). Toss until the wedges are well coated. Spread in an even layer onto the prepared pan.

4 Bake until browned and tender, 15 to 20 minutes. Using pot holders, remove the pan from the oven. Sprinkle potatoes with salt and serve hot. ⚠ HOT

FRESH TOMATO SALSA

Salsa is the Spanish word for "sauce." It can be cooked or fresh, chunky or blended until smooth. Salsas can be made with fruit, like mangoes, peaches, or papayas, or with tomatoes as in this classic Mexican version. Try it as a cool topping on spicy foods or as a dip with salty tortilla chips.

EQUIPMENT:

- Knife
- Cutting board
- Paring knife
- Medium bowl
- Spoon

MAKES **3** CUPS

INGREDIENTS:

4 ripe tomatoes

1 yellow bell pepper, seeded and chopped

4 green onions, trimmed and thinly sliced

¼ cup chopped fresh cilantro

1 small garlic clove, minced

1 small jalapeño, seeded and minced

1 tablespoon lemon juice

2 tablespoons olive oil

Salt and pepper

1 Using the paring knife, cut out the stem of each tomato. Cut each tomato in half. ⚠ SHARP

2 Using the knife, chop the tomato halves into small pieces. Scrape the tomatoes and juices into the medium bowl.

3 Add the bell pepper, green onions, cilantro, garlic, jalapeño, lemon juice, and oil. Season with salt and pepper and toss until mixed. Serve right away or cover and refrigerate up to 2 days.

Don't like the seeds? Use a spoon to scoop them out of the halved tomatoes.

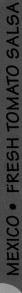

CLASSIC CHEESE QUESADILLAS

The word *quesadilla* means "little cheesy thing" in Spanish. Cheese is the only filling that all quesadillas have in common. In Mexico, they can be filled with just about anything and are often sold at street markets. In some places, they are even filled with a fungus grown on corn called *huitlacoche*.

EQUIPMENT:

- Jelly roll pan
- Aluminum foil
- Pastry brush
- Wire cooling rack
- Metal spatula
- Knife
- Cutting board

MAKES **4** SERVINGS

INGREDIENTS:

1½ tablespoons vegetable oil

4 large (8-inch/20-cm) flour tortillas

2 cups shredded cheddar cheese

To serve: sour cream, Fresh Tomato Salsa (see page 98), and Guacamole (see next page)

1 Arrange the oven rack in the middle of the oven. Heat the oven to 425°F (220°C). Line the jelly roll pan with foil.

2 Evenly brush one side of each tortilla with oil. Place one tortilla, oiled side down, on the prepared jelly roll pan. Evenly scatter ⅓ cup of the cheese over one half of the tortilla. Fold the uncovered half over the cheese and press gently. Repeat with remaining tortillas and cheese.

3 Bake until puffed and light brown on top, about 7 minutes. Using potholders, move the pan to the cooling rack. Using the metal spatula, turn the quesadillas over and press down slightly. Return the pan to the oven. Cook until the tortillas are light brown and the cheese has melted, about 3 minutes. ⚠ HOT

4 Using pot holders, remove the pan from the oven. Using the spatula, move the quesadillas to a cutting board and cut each one into 3 wedges. Serve hot. ⚠ SHARP

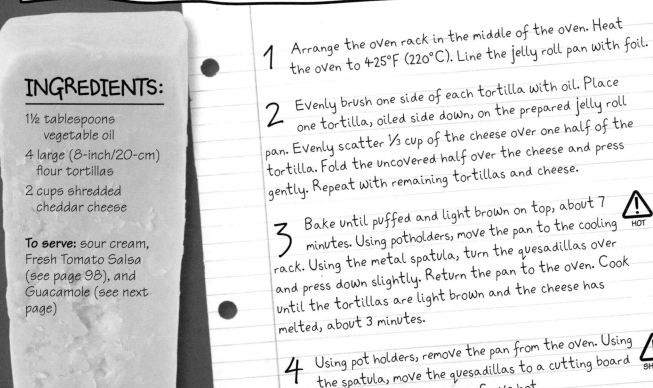

Guacamole

Here's another easy and delicious Mexican dip! Cut 3 ripe avocados in half, working around the pit. Using a spoon, remove the pit. Scoop the flesh into a medium bowl. Dice 1 tomato and add to the avocado. Add 1 minced garlic clove, 1 tablespoon fresh lime juice, 3 thinly sliced green onions, and 2 tablespoons minced fresh cilantro. Season with salt. Mix, lightly mashing the avocado with the spoon. Serve immediately or cover the surface directly with plastic wrap and refrigerate up to 1 day.

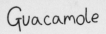

SHARP

JICAMA SLAW

EQUIPMENT:

- Zester
- Vegetable peeler
- Knife
- Cutting board
- Box grater
- Medium bowl

Jicama is a tuber (like potatoes) native to Mexico, where it's been eaten for centuries. It can be served cooked, but usually it's just shredded and mixed with a dressing, as it is in this recipe. You can adjust the chili powder if you like your slaw more or less spicy.

INGREDIENTS:

1 medium jicama, peeled

2 carrots, peeled

4 green onions, trimmed and thinly sliced

1 teaspoon finely chopped orange zest

½ cup fresh orange juice

2 tablespoons vegetable oil

½ teaspoon chili powder

Salt and pepper

1 Cut the jicama in half. Hold the grater firmly with one hand. Hold one of the jicama halves in the other hand and carefully slide it down over the large holes. Continue until both halves are shredded. ⚠ SHARP

2 Scoop up the shredded jicama and move to the bowl. Shred the carrots in the same way and add to the jicama.

3 Add the green onions, orange zest, orange juice, oil, chili powder, salt, and pepper to the bowl. Toss until well mixed. Serve immediately or cover and refrigerate up to 2 days.

Move jicama slowly on down the side of the grater, keeping your fingers back.

MEXICAN CHOCOLATE PUDDING

This creamy dessert is made with Mexican chocolate, which has cinnamon and sugar added to it. Mexican chocolate is often mixed with hot milk and served for breakfast with crispy doughnuts called *churros*. It's also delicious cold, as in this rich and easy-to-make pudding.

EQUIPMENT:

- Knife
- Cutting board
- Medium saucepan
- Whisk
- Small serving bowls
- Plastic wrap

MAKES 4 SERVINGS

INGREDIENTS:

¼ cup cornstarch

3 tablespoons sugar

2 cups milk

6 ounces (150 g) Mexican chocolate, chopped

2 tablespoons butter, cut into small pieces

1   In the medium saucepan, combine the cornstarch and the sugar. Whisking constantly, slowly add the milk. Add the chopped chocolate.

2   Set the pan over medium heat. Cook, whisking constantly, until the sauce is beginning to boil. ⚠ HOT Continue whisking and boil 1 minute.

3   Using pot holders, move the pan from the heat and whisk in the butter.

4   Carefully pour pudding into small serving bowls. Cover each one with plastic wrap. Press the plastic directly onto the surface to prevent a skin from forming. Refrigerate until cold, about 1 hour.

No Mexican chocolate? Mix 6 oz (150 g) semisweet chocolate, ¼ cup sugar, and ½ tsp cinnamon.

Chocolate

Chocolate begins with cocoa beans, which grow in pods on trees in moist, tropical climates. The beans are ground into a bitter-tasting paste called "chocolate liquor." You can taste this in bittersweet and semi-sweet chocolate, which have 55–72% chocolate liquor. These are the kinds of chocolate most often used for baking. Most chocolate we eat has less than half chocolate liquor, and contains sugar and cocoa butter for sweetness and texture. Milk chocolate also contains milk. White chocolate is not really chocolate at all, because it contains no chocolate liquor. It's actually a mixture of sugar, cocoa butter, and milk solids. Neither white nor milk chocolate can be substituted for semisweet chocolate in recipes.

Cinnamon-Sugar Tortilla Crisps

Tortillas for dessert? These crunchy snacks go well with Mexican Chocolate Pudding. Heat the oven to 375°F (190°C). In a small bowl, mix ½ cup sugar and 1 teaspoon ground cinnamon. In a small microwave-safe bowl, microwave 3 tablespoons butter until melted, about 20 seconds. Arrange 5 flour tortillas on a work surface. Brush with butter and sprinkle evenly with cinnamon-sugar. Cut each into wedges and arrange on cookie sheets. Bake until golden brown, about 10 minutes. Cool completely, then serve with dessert.

⚠ ELECTRIC

⚠ HOT

⚠ SHARP

JAMAICAN JERK CHICKEN

EQUIPMENT:

- Knife
- Cutting board
- Broiler pan
- Aluminum foil
- Medium bowl
- Tongs

"Jerk" refers to a Jamaican seasoning mix that's rubbed on meat, chicken, seafood, or veggies before grilling. Its sweet and spicy flavor comes from spices such as cinnamon and allspice. The heat comes from Scotch bonnet peppers, which are among the hottest chiles in the world. In this version, we use cayenne—it's just as tasty (and a little easier to find).

INGREDIENTS:

2 tablespoons vegetable oil

3 tablespoons firmly packed brown sugar

1½ teaspoons salt

¾ teaspoon ground cinnamon

¼ teaspoon dried thyme

¼ teaspoon ground allspice

⅛ teaspoon ground cayenne pepper

4 boneless, skinless chicken breast halves (about 1 pound/450 g)

To serve: Mango Salsa (see next page)

1 Arrange the oven rack in the upper third of the oven. Preheat the broiler to high. Line the broiler pan with foil.

2 In the medium bowl, stir together the oil, brown sugar, salt, cinnamon, thyme, allspice, and cayenne. Add the chicken breasts to the bowl, and toss to coat.

3 Arrange the chicken on the prepared pan. Scrape any remaining spices from the bowl onto the chicken.

4 Broil 6 minutes. Remove the pan from the oven and set on the cooling rack.
HOT

5 Using tongs, turn the chicken over. Return the pan to the oven and broil until the chicken is browned, about 5 to 7 minutes. Using pot holders, remove the pan from the oven. Serve hot with the Mango Salsa.

Mango Salsa

Fruit salsas are popular in the West Indies, because fruits like mango and pineapple grow so well there. Carefully cut 2 large mangoes in half, around the pit. Scoop out the flesh and cut up into small pieces. In a medium bowl, combine the mango with ¼ cup diced red bell pepper, ¼ cup diced red onion, ¼ cup chopped cilantro, 1 teaspoon minced jalapeño, 1 tablespoon lime juice, salt, and pepper. Cover and refrigerate until serving.

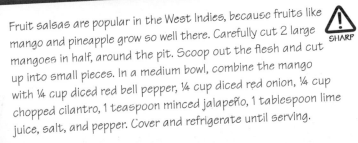

⚠ SHARP

TOSTONES

EQUIPMENT:

- Knife
- Cutting board
- Plate
- Paper towels
- Large skillet
- Tongs
- Plastic wrap
- Flat-bottomed glass

Grown throughout the Caribbean, plantains look like large bananas, but are less sweet and much starchier. They are often cooked like potatoes would be elsewhere. This dish (pronounced tohs-TOH-nays) is a favorite way to cook them, especially in Cuba and the Dominican Republic.

INGREDIENTS:

¾ cup vegetable oil

2 large green plantains, peeled and cut into 1-inch (2.5-cm) pieces

Coarse salt

1 Line a large plate with paper towels. Heat ½ cup oil in a large skillet over medium heat. Add 5 pieces of plantain. Cook until golden brown on the bottom, about 3 minutes. ⚠ HOT

2 Using tongs, turn the plantains over. Cook until golden brown on the bottom, about 3 minutes. Remove the plantains to the paper towel–lined plate. Repeat with remaining plantains.

3 Let the plantains cool slightly. Put a plantain between two pieces of plastic wrap. Using the bottom of the glass, flatten to about ½-inch (1.25-cm) thick. Repeat with remaining plantains.

4 Add the remaining oil to the oil in the skillet and heat over medium heat. Add 4 smashed plantains. Cook until golden brown on the bottom, about 2 minutes. ⚠ HOT

5 Turn the plantains. Cook until golden brown on the bottom, about 2 minutes. Remove the plantains to the paper towel-lined plate. Repeat with remaining plantains. Sprinkle with salt and serve immediately.

CUBAN BLACK BEAN SOUP

MAKES 6 SERVINGS

EQUIPMENT:

- Knife
- Cutting board
- Colander
- Blender
- Medium saucepan

Frijoles negros, or black beans, are a staple food in Caribbean and South American countries. They are usually served with rice or plantains (see opposite page) or in flavorful soups and stews like this one.

INGREDIENTS:

3 (15-ounce) cans black beans, rinsed and drained

1 (14½-ounce) can chopped tomatoes, NOT drained

2 tablespoons vegetable oil

1¼ cups diced cooked ham

1 onion, chopped

2 garlic cloves, minced

¾ teaspoon ground cumin

½ teaspoon dried oregano

Salt and pepper

3 cups water

To serve: Sour cream and cilantro sprigs

1 Put the beans and tomatoes (juice, too) in the blender (you may need to do this in batches). Process until almost smooth. Set aside. **ELECTRIC !**

2 Heat the oil in a medium saucepan over medium heat. Add the ham and onion. Cook, stirring frequently, until onion is soft and light brown around the edges, about 5 minutes. **HOT !**

3 Add the garlic, cumin, and oregano. Season with salt and pepper. Cook, stirring, about 1 minute.

4 Stir in beans and tomatoes. Add 3 cups water and bring to a boil. Reduce heat to low and simmer until thickened, about 20 minutes. Serve hot with sour cream and cilantro sprigs.

Flatbreads Around the World

Made of dough or batter, flatbread appears around the world as wraps, crackers, and even plates! Flatbreads usually have a mild flavor, but fillings can turn them into anything from a hearty breakfast to a salty snack to a delicious dessert. Check out how cultures around the world use native cooking techniques and local flavors to make these treats their own.

Johnnycakes, which were once a Native American dish, are sometimes cooked over a campfire.

FLOUR TORTILLAS

2 cups all-purpose flour, plus more for sprinkling
½ cup vegetable shortening
¾ cup warm water
1½ teaspoons salt

1. Mix the ingredients in a medium bowl until a dough forms. Turn out and knead for 1 minute. Divide into 8 balls.

2. Heat a heavy skillet over medium heat. ⚠ HOT

3. Sprinkle flour on your work surface and rolling pin. Roll each ball into a 6-inch round. (Don't worry if they're not perfectly round.) If the dough sticks to the work surface, sprinkle with flour.

4. Place 1 round in the hot pan. Cook, turning once, until bubbles pop up on each side, about 2 minutes per side.

5. Remove from the pan and wrap in a clean towel. Repeat, stacking the cooked tortillas in the towel.

Tortillas have been made in Latin America since pre-Columbian times. Made of cornmeal or flour, they are thin breads that are cooked on a very hot pan called a comal. Tortillas are wrapped around fillings (meat, vegetables, cheese) for breakfast, lunch, and dinner.

MEXICO

CHILE

Pancito ("little bread" in Spanish) is popular in Chile and other parts of South America. Made from flour, water, sugar, and yeast, it is served for breakfast with hot coffee or tea.

SWEDEN

Knackebröd is a crisp bread made with rye flour. The dough is rolled thin, scored, and baked. They're served with soup or eaten as a snack.

Blini are eaten all year in Russia, but are especially popular during the spring festival Maslenitsa.

Crêpes are thin pancakes made from flour, eggs, milk, and butter. Crêpes are eaten both as a main course and for dessert.

FRANCE

Langos are made from potatoes and are often sold at fairs. They are deep-fried and usually smeared with garlic butter.

HUNGARY

To make **scallion pancakes**, rice-flour dough is flattened, topped with scallions, and rolled into a log. The log is shaped into a coil, flattened again, and fried.

CHINA

Chapati is made with wheat flour, water, and salt. It's cooked in a very hot dry pan. It's used to sop up stews or curries or like scoops to pick up chunks of meat.

INDIA

Middle Eastern **lavash** dough is slapped against the wall of an oven called a *tonir* to bake.

Injera is made with teff (a tall Ethiopian grass) and water. Injera is used as a plate for stews or salads. Pieces of the "plate" are torn off and used like spoons.

ETHIOPIA

AUSTRALIA

Damper, a traditional Australian outback bread, is baked on the campfire, first on top of the coals and then covered with ashes to finish.

United States and Canada

The people of the United States and Canada are as diverse as the foods they eat. Most dishes here can be traced to either American Indian traditions or immigrant influences from other parts of the world. With a large land area and climate range, this region boasts a variety of native foods, from corn and maple syrup to blueberries, cranberries, and turkey.

The snow-covered peak of Mount Rainier in Washington state

ARCTIC
OCEAN

Canada

Canada has the second-largest land area of any country, so the climate is different depending on where you go. The food has been influenced by French and English settlers and by the native tribes that still call Canada home. Maple trees grow very well here, so maple syrup is a staple. (There is even a maple leaf on the Canadian flag.)

New England and the Northeast

The first part of the country to be colonized, this region's history is very colorful, as is the cooking. Every state in the Northeast (except Vermont) has a coastline, so fresh seafood is popular here. Oysters, clams, and lobster are just three kinds that you will find in abundance. The climate is ideal for farming, so fruit and vegetable stands are common, even in large cities.

C A N A D A

Western and Northwestern states

The climate here varies from rainy in Washington and Oregon to nearly always sunny in the southern part of California. These states are all on the Pacific Ocean, so seafood is plentiful. Asian immigrants influenced the cooking style, which focuses on the freshness of the ingredients.

U N I T E D   S T A T E S
O F   A M E R I C A

ATLANTIC
OCEAN

PACIFIC
OCEAN

Southeastern states

Dishes like collard greens were originally brought to America by African slaves. In Louisiana, Cajun and Creole foods also have Spanish, African, and French influences. Floridians enjoy Cuban and Caribbean dishes like black bean soup. Sweet Georgia peaches are an example of the plentiful fruit in this warm region, while the Carolinas and Tennessee are known for their barbecue.

Southwestern states

These states were once Mexican and Spanish colonies, and the culture and food show that. Texas cooking ranges from barbecued beef to Mexican-style dishes like tacos and enchiladas to German-influenced food like sausages. New Mexican cooking uses a lot of the green chile native to the area.

The Midwest

Called the "breadbasket of the world," this region is home to miles and miles of flat farmland. You'll find lots of grains, milk, and cheese here, as well as dishes brought over by German and Scandinavian settlers.

JAMBALAYA

EQUIPMENT:

- Knife
- Cutting board
- Large skillet with a lid
- Tongs
- Plate
- Wooden spoon

This classic Louisiana dish is a lot like Spanish *paella*. Some think that its name comes from the Spanish word *jamon* (ham), because the recipe often includes ham. Others think it came from the Creole words *jhamba* (gift) and *laya* (rice).

INGREDIENTS:

2 tablespoons oil

2 boneless, skinless chicken breast halves (about ½ pound/225 g), cut in half to make 4 pieces

2 links (½ pound/225 g) andouille sausage, cut into ½-inch (1.25-cm) coins

1 onion, chopped

1 green bell pepper, chopped

2 celery stalks, thinly sliced

1 cup long grain white rice

2 garlic cloves, minced

Salt and pepper

½ teaspoon dried thyme

1 (14½-ounce) can diced tomatoes (NOT drained)

1 cup frozen sliced okra

6 ounces (170 g) raw jumbo shrimp, peeled and deveined

1 Heat the oil in the large skillet over medium-high heat.  Add the chicken and cook until browned, 4 to 5 minutes. Using the tongs, turn the chicken and cook until browned, 4 to 5 minutes. Move the chicken to a plate and set aside.

2 Reduce the heat to medium. Add the sausage, onion, pepper, and celery. Cook, stirring frequently, until just tender, about 4 minutes.

3 Add the rice, garlic, ¾ teaspoon salt, and thyme to the skillet. Season with pepper. Stir until blended.

4 Add the tomatoes and their juice and 1¼ cup water. Bring to a boil. Stir frequently, scraping up any brown bits from the skillet.

5 Add the chicken and reduce the heat to low. Cover and simmer until the rice is barely tender, about 15 minutes. Carefully remove the lid. Scatter the okra and the shrimp over the top. Put the lid back on.

6 Simmer until the rice is tender and the shrimp is cooked through, about 5 minutes. Turn off the heat and carefully remove the lid. Gently toss the mixture to combine. Serve hot.

Creole Versus Cajun

Louisiana is known for two distinct cultures: Cajun and Creole. *Cajun* comes from the word *Acadian*, which refers to the French Canadians who fled Canada when the British and French went to war. Many Cajuns ended up in rural Louisiana, and Cajun cooking is "country" food: hearty one-pot meals made from local ingredients. It's often mixed with rice to feed more people. Creoles are descended from French and Spanish settlers who moved to New Orleans. Creole food combines local ingredients with classic French cooking styles. Both Cajun and Creole cooking use the "holy trinity" of bell pepper, onion, and celery.

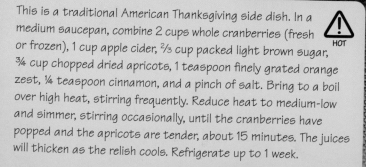

Cranberry-Apricot Relish

This is a traditional American Thanksgiving side dish. In a medium saucepan, combine 2 cups whole cranberries (fresh or frozen), 1 cup apple cider, 2/3 cup packed light brown sugar, 3/4 cup chopped dried apricots, 1 teaspoon finely grated orange zest, 1/4 teaspoon cinnamon, and a pinch of salt. Bring to a boil over high heat, stirring frequently. Reduce heat to medium-low and simmer, stirring occasionally, until the cranberries have popped and the apricots are tender, about 15 minutes. The juices will thicken as the relish cools. Refrigerate up to 1 week.

⚠ HOT

SOUTHERN-STYLE CORNBREAD

When European settlers arrived on American shores, they were introduced to corn and cornmeal by the natives. As settlers moved south and west, the recipes became more regional. Northern cornbreads are generally sweeter and richer than those made in the south, which have a drier texture.

EQUIPMENT:

- 8-inch (20-cm) glass baking dish
- Medium bowl
- Whisk
- Rubber spatula
- Toothpick
- Wire cooling rack

MAKES
9
PIECES

INGREDIENTS:

3 tablespoons butter, melted, plus extra for greasing dish

1⅓ cups cornmeal (medium-fine grind)

⅔ cup all-purpose flour

¼ cup sugar

2½ teaspoons baking powder

½ teaspoon salt

1¼ cups buttermilk

1 large egg

1 Arrange the oven rack in the middle of the oven. Heat the oven to 400°F (200°C). Lightly grease the baking dish with butter.

2 In a medium bowl, whisk the cornmeal, flour, sugar, baking powder, and salt. In a small bowl, whisk the buttermilk, melted butter, and egg until blended. Pour the buttermilk mixture over the cornmeal mixture. Mix just until blended.

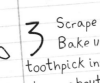

3 Scrape the batter into the baking dish. Bake until the edges are browned and a toothpick inserted near the center comes out clean, about 25 minutes. ⚠ HOT

4 Using pot holders, move the baking dish to the cooling rack. Let the cornbread cool at least 20 minutes. Cut into squares and serve warm or at room temperature.

APPLE-OATMEAL CRUMBLE

EQUIPMENT:

- Knife
- Cutting board
- 2 medium bowls
- Whisk
- 8-inch (20-cm) glass baking dish
- Wire cooling rack

While apples are indeed a big part of North American folklore thanks to Johnny Appleseed, apples are grown in other countries as well. Japan is where Fuji apples were first grown, and Gala apples come from New Zealand. But this warm treat (and Thanksgiving favorite) is All-American.

INGREDIENTS:

For the oatmeal topping:

1 cup all-purpose flour

½ cup firmly packed brown sugar

½ cup old-fashioned rolled oats

Pinch of salt

8 tablespoons butter, cut into 8 pieces and at room temperature

For the apple filling:

4 large apples (about 2 pounds/900 g), peeled, cored, and cut into thin (½-inch/2.5-cm) wedges

¼ cup firmly packed brown sugar

¾ teaspoon ground cinnamon

1 Preheat the oven to 375°F (190°C).

2 In the medium bowl, whisk flour, brown sugar, oatmeal, and salt. Add the butter pieces and toss until butter is blended in. (The mixture should clump together when you pinch it.) Refrigerate.

3 In another bowl, combine the apple slices, brown sugar, and cinnamon. Toss until the apples are evenly coated.

4 Spread the apple mixture into the baking dish. Scrape in any juices from the bowl.

5 Using your fingers, break apart the chilled topping into small clumps and scatter over the apples.

6 Bake until the topping is golden and the apples are tender, 45 to 50 minutes. Using pot holders, move the baking dish to the cooling rack. Let cool at least 15 minutes. Serve warm. ⚠ HOT

Make sure the topping and the apples are in even layers in the baking dish.

Johnny Appleseed

There really was a Johnny Appleseed! His real name was John Chapman and he was born in Massachusetts in 1774. Johnny was a big fan of apples and made the planting and sharing of apple trees his life's work. He planted his first orchards in western New York and Pennsylvania. As explorers and settlers moved west, Johnny moved along with them, planting new apple orchards along the way. Some land companies required settlers to plant apple trees in order to get the deed to the land where they were living. Luckily, Johnny was there to pass along seeds and trees. Thanks to Johnny's work, apples are still grown all over North America.

CRISPY PARMESAN BAKED COD

Large schools of cod live in the Atlantic Ocean off the coast of North America. Codfishing has been a major industry in the United States and Canada for many years. If you've tried fish sticks, you've probably had this mild-flavored white fish. This recipe is similar because of the breading, but much tastier.

EQUIPMENT:

- Knife
- Cutting board
- Small jelly roll pan
- Aluminum foil
- Pie plate
- Fork

MAKES 4 SERVINGS

1 Arrange the oven rack in the upper third of the oven. Heat the oven to 425°F (220°C). Line the jelly roll pan with foil and spray lightly with nonstick cooking spray.

2 In the pie plate, stir together the bread crumbs, Parmesan, parsley, thyme, salt, and pepper. Pour the butter over the mixture. Toss with a fork until all the crumbs are moist.

3 Fold over any thinner pieces of fish so all the pieces are about the same thickness. Spread the mustard evenly over the top and sides of each fish strip.

4 Press the coated sides of the fish strips into the crumbs. Use a fork to turn the strips over to make a thick coating of crumbs. Place the fish crumb side up on the prepared pan. Sprinkle the fish with some of the leftover crumbs.

5 Bake until the crumbs are golden brown and ⚠ HOT the fish is cooked through, 10 to 12 minutes. Using pot holders, remove the pan from the oven. Serve hot.

INGREDIENTS:

Nonstick cooking spray

¾ cup dried bread crumbs

⅓ cup grated Parmesan cheese

1 tablespoon chopped fresh parsley

1 teaspoon chopped fresh thyme leaves

½ teaspoon salt

¼ teaspoon pepper

4 tablespoons butter, melted

1¼ pounds (565 g) fresh cod, cut into 1½-inch (4-cm)-wide strips

2 tablespoons Dijon mustard

Use your fingertips to press the crumb mixture onto the fish so it's well coated.

Ranch Dressing

This dressing is delicious on any kind of lettuce, or used as a dip for fresh vegetables. In a small bowl, whisk together ½ cup buttermilk, ½ cup mayonnaise, and 2 teaspoons lemon juice. Add 3 tablespoons finely chopped green onions, ¼ teaspoon minced garlic, 3 tablespoons chopped fresh parsley, ¼ teaspoon salt, and ¼ teaspoon pepper. Whisk until well blended. Refrigerate for 30 minutes or up to 3 days before serving.

SUMMER SUCCOTASH

This stew, originally called *msikwatash*, was created by the Narragansett tribe. During the summer, tribes ate mostly fresh beans, corn, and squash in dishes like this one. (The Iroquois called these ingredients "the three sisters" and planted them together.) In the winter, tribes ate dried corn, berries, and meat prepared during the warmer months.

EQUIPMENT:

- Knife
- Cutting board
- Plate
- Paper towels
- Large skillet
- Tongs

MAKES **4** SERVINGS

1 Line the plate with paper towels.

2 Arrange the bacon slices in a large skillet over medium-low heat. Cook, turning with the tongs, until crispy, about 6 minutes. Move the bacon to the paper towel–lined plate. Keep the bacon drippings in the skillet.

 HOT

3 Add the red pepper and garlic to the pan. Cook over medium-low heat, stirring, until tender, about 3 minutes. Add the zucchini, corn, and lima beans. Cook, stirring, about 2 minutes.

4 Add the tomato. Cook, stirring, until the vegetables are tender, about 8 minutes.

5 Crumble the cooked bacon into the skillet. Stir in the basil, salt, and pepper. Serve hot or at room temperature.

INGREDIENTS:

5 slices bacon (about ¼ pound/112 g)

1 red bell pepper, chopped

1 garlic clove, minced

1 zucchini, cut in half lengthwise and thinly sliced

2 cups frozen corn

¼ pound (112 g) frozen baby lima beans

1 tomato, seeded and chopped

3 tablespoons chopped fresh basil

Salt and pepper

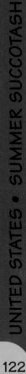

Corn

Like rice grown in Asia, corn is a wild grass that people have been eating for centuries. Corn was probably the most important food for the American Indians, and they ate it year-round. During the summer, they ate fresh corn right off the stalk. They also set aside a large amount of corn to dry and store for the winter months, when food was more scarce. They stored ears of corn and cut off the kernels to eat whole. Dried corn was also ground and used to make breads and puddings. Corn is still a very important food all over the world. It is the main ingredient in all kinds of dishes, including cornbread, tamales, tortillas, and stews like succotash.

CANADIAN BUTTER TARTS

Canada is home to many delicious traditional dishes. In Vancouver, you can enjoy Pacific salmon and even some Inuit cooking. In Quebec, you'll be served *poutine*, a dish of fried potatoes and gravy. In Ontario, where maple syrup is produced, these tarts are a favorite.

EQUIPMENT:

- 12-cup muffin pan
- 3½-inch (8.75-cm) round cookie cutter
- Medium bowl
- Whisk
- Wire cooling rack
- Table knife

MAKES **12** TARTS

INGREDIENTS:

Nonstick cooking spray

All-purpose flour (for rolling)

2 pre-made pie crusts, at room temperature

¾ cup maple syrup

4 tablespoons butter, melted

⅓ cup firmly packed light brown sugar

½ teaspoon vanilla extract

2 large eggs

⅔ cup raisins

1 Arrange the oven rack in the bottom third of the oven and heat to 375°F (190°C). Spray muffin cups with the nonstick spray (even if you have a nonstick pan).

2 Sprinkle a little flour over the work surface. Unroll a pie crust and lay it flat on the floured surface. Using the cookie cutter, cut out 6 rounds. Repeat with the second crust for a total of 12 rounds.

3 Using your fingers, gently press rounds into the bottom and about ¾ of the way up the sides of the muffin cups.

4 In a medium bowl, whisk together the syrup, melted butter, brown sugar, and vanilla. Add the eggs and whisk just until blended.

5 Put a few raisins in each crust. Pour the filling evenly over the raisins.

6 Bake until the crust is golden brown and the filling is puffed and jiggles a little when the pan is nudged. Using pot holders, move the pan to the cooling rack.

HOT

7 Let cool 5 minutes, then gently run a table knife between the crust and the muffin cups. Cool completely, then lift the tarts out of the cups with the tip of the knife. Serve at room temperature.

Maple Syrup

Maple syrup is made from the sap that drips out of maple trees. Maple trees grow all over the world. But only the ones in climates with long, cold winters like New England and Canada produce sap. Sugar season is at the end of winter when the days are a little warmer but nighttime temperatures are still freezing. Farmers drill holes into the trunks and hang buckets underneath to catch the dripping sap. The sap is brought to "sugar shacks" and boiled for hours. When most of the water has boiled away, you have maple syrup! It takes 30 to 50 gallons of sap to make 1 gallon of syrup.

Maple Butter

Maple-flavored butter is great on toast, pancakes, waffles, or even baked sweet potatoes! Beat 8 tablespoons (room-temperature) butter until smooth and fluffy. Add 1 to 2 tablespoons maple syrup and beat until blended. Serve immediately or store in the fridge or freezer.

ELECTRIC

Index

Author's note

A zillion thanks to Alissa Smith, my trusted kitchen assistant, whose effervescent attitude never waivered throughout countless tests and re-tests. My heartfelt and continued appreciation goes to a true research goddess and friend, Li Agen. And last but hardly least, my deepest thanks goes to Patty Brown, Sara Newberry, and the terrific team at Downtown Bookworks, as well as the entire staff at DK. Teamwork at its finest!

Publisher's note

DK Publishing would like to thank the following for helping make this book ready to serve: Pamela Duncan Silver, Vivian Liu, Alison Attenborough, Jamie Kim, and Tamami Mihara. And especially our models: Jeremy Berlinski, Naomi Christiansen, Zoe Fox, Nehal Gajjar, Elizabeth Gallagher, Alex Gong, Justin Llavina, Morris Katz, Eliane Mitchell, Scotia Rollins, Kofi Samuels, Emily Stearns, Julia Rose Stiblich, and Raymond Walther.

Photo Credits

DK Publishing thanks the following for their kind permission to reproduce photographs and illustrations:

pp. 6–7 Taj Mahal: Getty Images. Tamales: Jupiter Images. Pupusas: Jupiter Images. Gyozas: Jupiter Images. Empanadas: Jupiter Images.
p. 19 Abigail Johnson Dodge: Courtesy of *Fine Cooking Magazine*.
p. 21 Japanese Temple: Getty Images.
p. 23 Sushi: DK Images.
p. 33 Taj Mahal/Camel: Getty Images.
p. 43 Spices: DK Images.
pp. 44–45 Tamales: Jupiter Images. Pupusas: Jupiter Images. Gyozas: Jupiter Images. Empanadas: Jupiter Images.
p. 46 Desert: Getty Images.
p. 53 Olives: DK Images.
p. 56 Olive Oil: DK Images.

pp. 70–71 Stilton: Jupiter Images. Gouda: DK Images. Paneer: DK Images. Feta: DK Images.
p. 73 Cottages: Getty Images.
p. 81 Paprika: DK Images.
p. 91 Tea: DK Images.
p. 92 Caribbean Beach: Getty Images.
pp. 110–111 Johnny Cakes: Jupiter Images. Lavash: DK Images. Blini: DK Images.
p. 112 Mount Rainer: Jupiter Images.
p. 123 Corn: DK Images.

Maps on pages: 2–3, 6, 8–9, 20–21, 32–33, 44–45, 46–47, 70–71, 72–73, 92–93, 110–111, 112–113: DK Cartography.

Other illustrations by Bill Miller.